Who am I?

I am a man, just like you, a simple and needy person — in need of the mercy of God and of your prayers, because I have been given charge, without merit or choice on my part, of representing the Lord Jesus.

I am the Successor of St. Peter, the Apostle to whom the Lord gave the powers of directing and sanctifying the Church.

I am the Pope, which means the father of all.

I come to you in the name of the Lord, and I wish that when you look at me you would have your thoughts on Him, on Jesus, Who is present in my ministry.

(Words of Paul VI, Bogota, 1968)

the Sixth Paul

James V. Schall, S.J.

ALBA BOOKS

Library of Congress Catalog Card No. 77-71026
ISBN   0-8189-1147-6
© Alba House Communications,
Canfield, Ohio, 44406

Printed in the United States of America

The Author wishes to thank the Editors of WORLDVIEW and THE MONTH for allowing him to reprint material already published by them. Other material quoted is used with permission and details of sources are given at the end.

Photo Credits: Page 31, NC; page 71, Society for the Propagation of the Faith; other pages, Osservatore Romano

CONTENTS

Introduction		1
1.	Why Believe?	11
2.	The Pope's Mind	33
3.	Who Is the Priest?	57
4.	Life-Giving Pontiff	79
5.	Social Thinker	103
6.	Figure of Faith	125
Footnotes		161

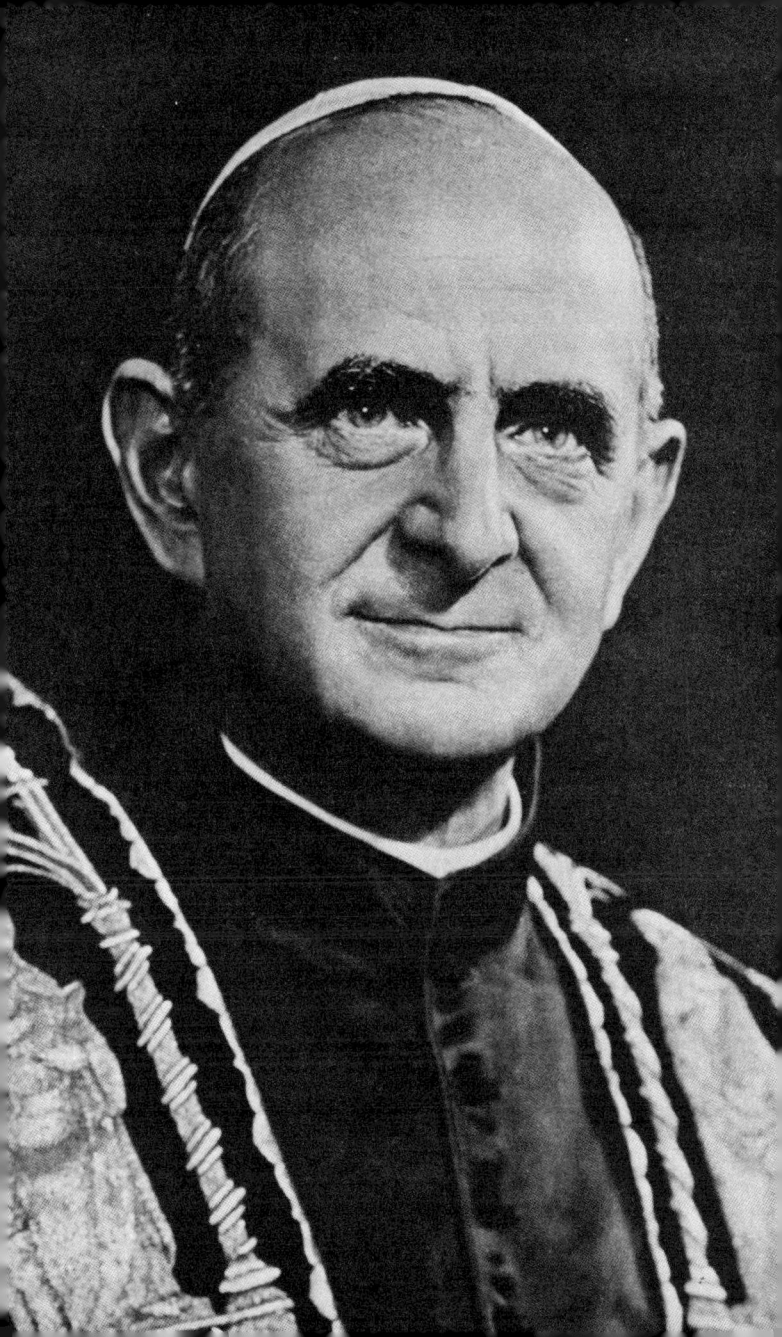

"Praised be God, the Father of our Lord Jesus Christ, the Father of mercies, and the God of all consolation! He comforts us in all our afflictions and thus enables us to comfort those who are in trouble, with the same consolation we have received from him. As we have shared much in the suffering of Christ, so through Christ do we share abundantly in his consolation. If we are afflicted, it is for your encouragement and salvation, and when we are consoled it is for your consolation, so that you may endure patiently the same sufferings we endure."

(St. Paul to the Corinthians: 2, 3-6)

Introduction

Few men and fewer Popes, have reached their Eightieth Birthday still in public office, still in control of their situation. What to do when one is eighty is no easy decision, since few men ever really expect to have to decide about their possibilities and their life at that age.

Leo XIII, to be sure, was almost eighty when he was elected Pope and he lasted another twenty or so years in one of the papacy's most productive periods. But old age is one of the prejudices of the modern world, the very institutions of which are designed to reduce, if not eliminate altogether, its influence. Ironically, the nations wherein old age in rule seems to be most in vigor and vogue are the marxist ones.

Paradoxically, the modern world is currently also against children. Eventually, and more rapidly than we might expect, we will be witnessing an aging population with an ever more crucial and agonizing conflict of generations, generations which do not firmly believe in the sanctity of life, young or old.

This eroding of the value and dignity of human life is a result Paul VI clearly foresaw. His old age can be taken as a symbol of his wisdom. Such is our time, I suspect, that few will acknowledge him to be prophetic even when he clearly is. The single most important thing he has done for mankind is to insist on the importance of every single human life, in whatever stage of its growth or decline.

The Pope has been in office since 1963. There is no way to recount and evaluate all of his varied efforts, what he has done well, what ill. The Church is not God, nor in Catholic doctrine is the Pope anything other than a human being. Yet, when we make the Church nothing *but* human, when we insist its leader is no different from the other four billion of us, we run into a kind of impasse, something not quite explicable in scientific terms.

Paul VI has been accused of many faults, a few vices even, while he has received far less praise than is his due. Just why this is so is itself a crucial question. He has been strikingly liberal and strikingly conservative—suggesting that he may be neither, or both, or that he has other sources of wisdom than those contained in these ideological adjectives of liberal and conservative.

He has made hard decisions, even against the weighty opinions of many of his academic or diplomatic advisors. Yet, often he has seemed too indecisive to make any decisions at all. He has a fine quality of not wanting to hurt or embarrass anyone, even those Catholics who clearly do not teach or practice what falls within Christian tradition. And yet such considerateness is often viewed as a weakness.

George A. Kelly, in a sympathetic and incisive essay, has reasoned this way: that the bad morale in the Church "may be due to the inability of the Pope to make his decisions stick or to select the kind of bishops who will do this for him."[1] Finding a middle way between graciousness and firmness has never been easy, especially for a Pope who must have both qualities.

Such American journals as *Newsweek* and *Time*, as Professor Hitchcock has carefully documented in a brilliant analysis, have often deliberately and persistently pictured Paul VI in a bad light because he did not rule the Church according to their presuppositions.[2] It is curious how much more infallibly the secular world speaks than does the papacy! And it is difficult indeed to know how to evaluate a Pope whose language and culture are Italian, whose broader vision is most often filtered through French. For better or worse, these Latin traditions are alien in many ways to those of the English-speaking world, a world which has its own presuppositions and prejudices equally difficult for others to comprehend.

But a Pope must read and speak some language, even if it be Urdu or Cantonese. Even should he speak ten languages, he will hardly begin to converse with most of the human race. And the problem of communication is by no means exclusive to the Holy See. Some effort must be made to look at him sympathetically, to see him through eyes that at least are not dogmatically hostile.

This is no easy thing to do. The complexity of the human world is such that no word or action will please everyone. If our only knowledge of what the Pope actually does or says is through the secular press, we can be fairly sure we will be hopelessly ill-informed. And still, it is so difficult to hear him in any other way.

Christians in the contemporary world have not been overly adept at assuring themselves of objective contact with their hierarchy. There is the Vatican Radio, to be sure, the *Acta Romana, L'Osservatore Romano, The Pope Speaks,* and various national and diocesan journals. But these are unavailable to most and, at best, bare echos and distant voices in the ears of the normal believer.

After years of living part time in Rome, I have never ceased to be amazed at the difference between what the Pope says, the impression he makes on actual people who see him, in comparison with the image of him among those who have never physically seen, read, or heard him. Some will maintain that if he said anything of value or interest, the world would know it, the word would get around. In part, this is true, but I am no longer quite so sure that the Holy Father receives anywhere near a fair hearing, even at times from his most faithful followers.

No doubt we can hear and read him if we desire to do so, if we demand it of ourselves and our media. But we do not. Hearing what the Church teaches is itself a spiritual problem. The Apostle Paul told us that faith comes through hearing. It is no accident that it is so hard to hear even a Pope!

On Paul VI's Eightieth birthday I do not intend to write another biography of him, still less a "criticism" of what he "should" have done. I believe he might have done some things better. I am sure he believes the same. I am also convinced he could have done many things worse.

For the most part, the most severe criticisms leveled against him were really not at Paul VI as Pope, but against what Christians were bound to believe anyway from their sources of faith for which he stood. There is a kind of persistent sanity in his words and sympathies. He betrays all the marks of the human, but on very many crucial issues, there is something of the Gates not standing against him, something in him protecting the best interests of mankind.

If I were God, I should not have chosen an obscure Italian to be Pope over and over again. But evidently this is better than a Committee or even a Council. Besides, if not an Italian, who? We would still end up with another human being from some other very narrow place, speaking some other language unknown to most men. Any Pope will be disliked by many for one reason or another. Even the good, Christianity has always known, will also be hated at times. Besides, the most popular pope was probably the one who preceded Paul VI —himself also an obscure Italian.

So what I should like to recall of this Pope, this Sixth Paul, are some stands he took, some dilemmas he faced, some abiding questions he had to handle again. (I say "again", since the human race does not have, from age to age, completely different problems touching it.) I want to suggest that within the context of the history of the papacy, Paul VI illuminated us in many ways. I want to insist first that a man occupies this office, one not without its humor. Indeed, the first approach to the subject of the Pope will not so much be about him, but about the papacy, our—or at least my—attitude towards it, how important it is to see this paradoxical office in this perplexing Church with the eyes of faith and of humor. Unless we realize this, we cannot really be Christians. And within this very human context, I also want to suggest that we cannot reduce all the activity and words of the papacy to the "merely human."

Beyond this, I want to pursue themes that are centered around the various ways in which "life" has been seen by Paul VI: intellectual, religious, and priestly; those problems of life that arise out of war, population, and development. Finally I want to say something about Paul's own view of the spiritual life, an amazing insight, in a way, into the meaning of Christianity itself. I do not doubt that each of these themes has behind it a view of theology and scripture that gives substance to the way the papacy treats modern problems, just as the criticisms leveled at the papacy for its views are also generally rooted in differing views of man and his destiny. Our times have been so largely social in emphasis and doctrine that we cannot easily see the abiding sense that this pope has often insisted on calling to our attention from the vantage point of his office and the wisdom of his experience.

This Pontiff has changed the papacy in more ways than we can count. He has been anything but a "prisoner in the Vatican," as many of his immediate predecessors considered themselves to be. He has travelled to the various continents. He has even introduced an age-limiting factor in the hierarchy. He has made non-Europeans more and more dominant among the bishops and cardinals. He has certainly asked himself about his own retirement should his health fail. He even may have wondered about removing the Vatican some place else should the whole political climate of Italy change radically (a move Pius XII at least considered during World War II for some of the Vatican offices). He has met most of the important political and religious leaders of his time. And his presence during most of the sessions of Vatican II made him Pope during one of the Church's most intensive periods of self-reflection and reform.

In each of the areas that I have selected to emphasize something of the contribution of Paul VI, I have attempted to place both him and the particular issue in some historical or personal context. I have tried to cite his own words enough to give some feeling for the man. I am interested in what is unique about Paul, but this uniqueness must also be seen as part of a more enduring process of the history of the Church and its meaning to the world.

Why Believe?

1

The Pope will always be either too anxious or fat, too deceptive or too jolly, too easy-going or too thin, too simple or too intelligent, too efficient or too boorish, too short or too tall. Does our faith depend upon these qualities of efficiency and likeability that the Pope may have? All modern thought believes in man as *he might be*. Faith believes in the existence of man *as he is*.

In approaching the contributions and works of Paul VI, I am going to begin in a rather indirect, even unusual way. Before anyone can speak of such a thing as a Pope, he must have some kind of attitude, some kind of an outlook on where this Church and this office fit into the sanity of things. Probably it is not unfair to say that any attempt to say anything rather positive about the record of the Pope will be greeted in many circles with skepticism, but it is precisely the skepticism of such circles that makes me think that he may be on the right path.

So I want to begin not immediately with him but with a kind of reflection on our times and where the meaning of faith and intelligence come before us. I am going to begin with the odd notion of "the papacy and humor." This is not a collection of papal jokes. Rather, I want to establish that Christianity is really about *men,* men who indeed share the joyous grace of God, yet men still in all they do.

Were the Church run directly by the Almighty, who would hesitate to believe in it? But the God we have does not operate that way. So when we think of a human being, one Giovanni Montini, who has been Pope for some years now, when we try to come to terms with his office and what he has taught us, we must begin somewhat further back, some place within our spirit that tells us what we can expect of reality and of faith. I will begin to talk about Paul VI by talking of a lot of strange and paradoxical notions we have about how it all fits together.

Faith and authority are, solemn and serious subjects. Yet, there is a danger, even a metaphysical danger in treating them so gravely and so soberly that all lightheartedness and all laughter must be excluded from their reality. I say "metaphysical danger" because both faith and authority are meant for human beings. It is the infallible mark of something humanly wrong when humor is excluded from any aspect of life. The human condition is, to be sure, serious. But it is also funny, sometimes very funny.

In spite of our various comedians; in spite of Art Buchwald, Charlie Brown, *Mad,* and *Punch;* in spite of Malcolm Muggeridge, the cartoonists in *The New Yorker,* and the Editorial writers of *The Economist,* we live in a generation that often has forgotten—perhaps may never have known—the delight of the human condition, even amidst its admitted tragedies.

A friend of mine was skiing some years ago in

the Austrian Alps with a group of American university students. As is the pleasant, immemorial custom after a day on the slopes, everyone who could still walk gathered in the evening to drink some beer, perhaps even to try some schnapps, to sing, to be together—the classic human scene for shouting, for joy, for sentimentality.

Among those students there were many guitars, many singers. Each took his turn singing, something personal, something meaningful. But after a couple of hours of this dirge atmosphere my unregenerate friend was dismayed. Finally, he protested: "Don't you have any happy and communal songs we can sing together? We're here to enjoy each other, to laugh and to roar!" "The world in which we live," he was firmly told, "is too serious for anything but sorrowful music."

What is striking about the university students in recent decades is that they can no longer enjoy a simple prank among themselves, nor even, it seems, bother to think one up. No longer is there to be time for anything but the serious issues of our days, days in which so many intellectuals preach doom. Men, it is implied, do not need a time to relax and a time to cheer.

Really? What profiteth it a man to gain the whole world and lose his sense of humor? Can we ever grow up, can we ever know what it is to be men if we do not know carefree days, if we do not roar and sing and shout together? Perhaps the greatest task of faith today is to save our ability to laugh, to protect us from the perfectionists and the doomsdayers.

Our times have seen millions of young people memorize the *Sayings of Mao-Tse-tung*. The level of forced indoctrination, not to mention the voluntary kind, is very high in the modern world. When the Chinese had a rule that seven hundred million people must read and believe the *Sayings* of Mao, it made about as much sense as requiring fifty million Englishmen to memorize Mother Goose. In fact, it made less sense. Mother Goose is at least worthwhile remembering, as Bruno Bettelheim has reminded us.[1]

The only appropriate response to such a law is laughter, with some fear perhaps as we realize what absolute states today can in fact make us read and hear. Yet, too many students, and not students alone, neither fear nor laugh, but ponder the newest ideologies without the experience of the human that keeps us sane. This has to be funny if we could only get away from ourselves far enough to see its absurdity.

The Blind Leading the Englishmen

There is a subtle, almost frightening relationship between the loss of laughter and the belief in a perfect world, the belief that governs, more than anything else, the visionaries of our time, the belief that is most opposed to Christianity and its institutions. This seems to have something to do with faith as well as with authority. Yet, the relationship may not be all that easy to explain.

Perhaps I might begin by saying that it is faith that makes laughter possible because it is faith that declares that it is all right to be a human being, a weak, sinful, somewhat improbable, usually awkward, wobbly human being. And, I might add, today it is only faith that still believes this.

All modern thought believes in man as *he might be*. Faith believes in the existence of man as *he is*. Behind the current controversy about population, development, and culture lies this gigantic, impossible dream that it is possible, even for God, to love men as they are. And men as they are, if we will take the time to notice it, are actually quite funny.

In recent years, the topic of the "crisis in the Church" has become a much publicized feature in the world press. It is usually discussed most vehemently and sagely by those who are either not in the Church or who are just about to leave it. One of the reasons for this phenomenon is the nature of modern mass media, or the ease with which private secrets are made public, or the publicity value of controversy.

But, however the crisis is described, one theme always predominates, that of the relation of visible authority to authentic faith, or more exactly, *how authority handles itself in accomplishing its mission*—if it has one, for that is also disputed. Whether it be population, ordination of women, or dealings with marxist governments, this problem recurs. We should be clear about the broader issues involved here. They do go to the very essence of the meaning of Christianity to mankind.

Writing in *Le Figaro Littéraire* several years ago,

Claude Jannoud justly noted the fascinating—and not to be passed over lightly—frequency with which writers and intellectuals outside the Church become involved and influential in ecclesiastical affairs.

> Evidently, one of the actual signs of crisis resides in the enormous interest that persons and organizations traditionally hostile to Catholicism or, better, strangers to it, suddenly accord to the problems of the Church in France. One would say that suddenly any kind of unbeliever or any dearly-beloved atheist or member of another church has arrogated to himself the right to decide what is good or bad for Catholics. But naturally, this shocking and absurd intrusion only has a credible value because it is founded on schismatic tendencies among certain Catholics.[2]

The Italian writer Virgilio Titone is even more harsh. He believes that modern religious opposition is so intellectually weak and silly that the only point of cohesion it can find is in attacking the papacy.

> The protagonists of today's confrontations do not care in the slightest to found a new reformed religion....
>
> They have need of the prestige and of the tradition of the Church that they combat and that, with its ancient hierarchical organization, represents the sole firm and secure point in the almost total bewilderment of modern religious sentiment.[3]

A similar situation, though on the level of practice, happened in Chicago where a group of black citizens, *mainly non-Catholics*, organized to insist before the Cardinal-Archbishop that a particular priest be immediately made pastor of one of the city's black parishes. The good prelate found himself caught in the impossible crossfire of episcopal authority, black dignity, human weaknesses, and the threat from other grounds.

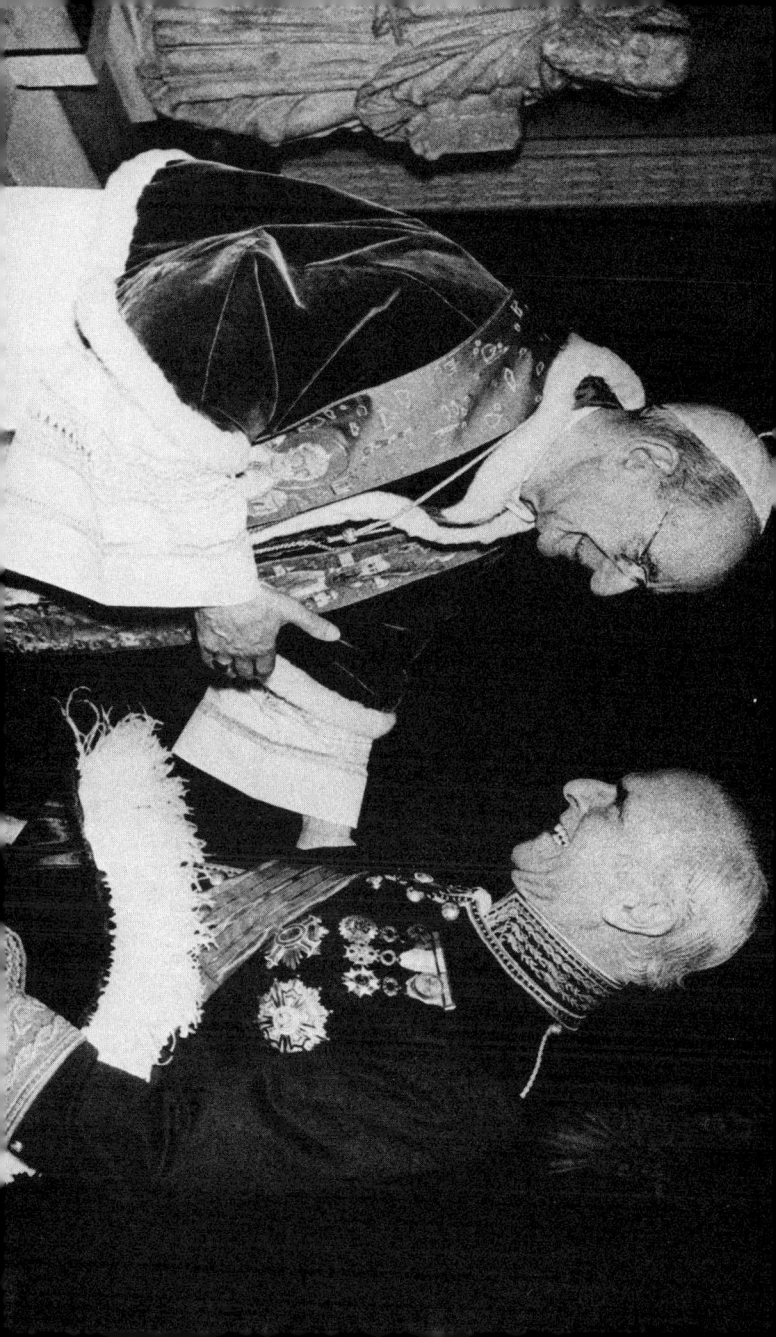

The way to resolve such problems of authority today is not as easy as it may once have been. In his *History of the English Church and People,* the Venerable Bede describes the resolution of a violent controversy between the English bishops and Augustine over the question of the date of Easter. When rational discourse finally failed, Augustine decided to resolve the struggle by a kind of holy tournament.

He brought in a blind Englishman and set him before the English prelates. But their prayers availed for nothing. Then the man was brought before Augustine who asked that he might be cured to bring "the light of spiritual grace to the minds of countless multitudes." Immediately he was healed and all admitted that Augustine had won the argument.

Yet, as if to show that even miracles are sometimes not enough Bede adds this delightful consequence: "The Britons admitted that his teaching was true and right, but said again that they could not abandon their customs without the consent and approval of their own people, and therefore asked that a second and fuller conference might be held!"

If Augustine, fortified by a miracle, had so much difficulty in winning an argument, we can perhaps find some sympathy for his inheritors centuries later as they, too, try to bring "the light of spiritual grace to the minds of countless multitudes." Indeed, the very question of whether there should be "countless multitudes" on this earth is one of the main problems these non-miraculous modern prelates have to answer.

A Preference for Hamburgers

The crucial question is: *do we or do we not believe solely because of the way in which religious authority goes about its appointed task?* Is it theologically necessary that the exercise of authority in the Church and its efficiency and excellence should be the *primary* cause of belief or unbelief? Can God not give authority to human beings who are by definition fallible and therefore also funny? Or must spiritual authority always, like Augustine, bring in a blind Englishman to restore his sight before we can believe?

Of course, I believe in the *"ecclesia semper reformanda."* And I am as frustrated as the next man by inefficiencies and by the petty weaknesses of religious authority. The Scribes and Pharisees of any age or organization deserve the bad publicity they get. But if the Vatican were run with the dispatch and smoothness with which Mr. McNamara used to run the Pentagon or the flair with which Mr. Kissinger ran the State Department, would that really make it more believable?

An American Methodist bishop once suggested that we might use hamburgers and soda pop for Communion if this were meaningful to the communicant. (For those who have a pessimistic view of history, this suggestion was bound to originate in America!)

Without suggesting that, on the same principles, the Italians should use pizza and the Japanese saki, the good bishop concluded: "We are determined not to continue doing the things that have no meaning in the modern world."[4] But if a piece of unleavened bread and some wine have no meaning for the modern world, will it suddenly be converted into the belief in the Real Presence when this is discovered under the species of a Big Mac and Coca-Cola? I confess some skepticism.

The very meaning of "Revelation" is that the world, modern or otherwise, does not have sufficient meaning in itself to discover his destiny to man. Something is revealed that the world by itself cannot explain. As Paul told Timothy, it is our function to pass on what the Lord has taught us. Admittedly, this seems like a most ineffective method to guarantee that this revelation will remain present among men. Yet it seems to have been the one chosen.

In his Introduction to *Christian Theology and Natural Science,* E. L. Mascall—perhaps the only modern theologian who still writes about the eternal mysteries with a quick wit and a dance in his eye—concludes with a plea for understanding between the scientists and the theologians. Then he finishes slyly: "For it is the scientists and the theologians that need to be brought together, not merely science and theology. And in any case, as Cardinal Gasquet remarked to Pius XI, we are none of us infallible." It is this sense of humanity and incongruity that makes the authority of a Pope and a cardinal believable.

Not Even the Dutch Need Like Him

Today, we no longer seem to have a world in which a cardinal can josh a Pope. Both must be perfect, both Pope and cardinal—if such a thing is even imaginable. An influential Italian weekly *L'Espresso* published once a long discussion on "The Drama in the Church." The format of this special supplement took the form of a round table exchange among *i piu celebri teologhi d'Europa* (the most noted European theologians).

The third section of the discussion dealt with the absorbing question of whether "disobedience is a sin." Unfortunately, the most celebrated theologians of Europe gave us no usable answer to this common problem. As the talks went on, the noted Dutch chaplain Jan van Kilsdonk compared the way the late Bishop Bekkers ran his diocese with the way Paul VI runs Christendom (or, to be sure, a small part of it). Bekkers was, in van Kilsdonk's view, a man who was (shades of Augustine!) "a miracle of humanity ... the incarnation of spiritual liberty both for believers and non-believers."

It is always difficult to compete with a miracle, let alone with an incarnation and predictably, Paul VI, did not make the grade: "If in Holland no one can say anything similar about Paul VI, it is because among us, every Catholic perceives in this Pope a timorous man, the incarnation of anxiety. Certainly, he is a most noble man, but this incredible anxiety seems to us the contrary of the faith."[5]

This is a remarkable statement and we should reflect on it if we are to understand the papacy and the Pope. If I understand it rightly—it misses the whole point of the papacy, if not the incarnation itself, namely: Is it possible for a mere man,

Giovanni Montini, to be Pope? Must he be someone besides himself with his own personality so that the Dutch and the rest of us could believe in his authority?

Is the essence of this authority any more believable to the modern world if a superman with no anxieties is on the throne of St. Peter's, than the Eucharist would be if transsubstantiated hamburgers formed the Holy Communion? Could God have set up such a system in which the salvation of men depends on men—to use Leo XIII's phrase? Was God bound to have established a method of theocratic government that had no dependences or no limitations caused by the characteristics—anxious or liberal, kindly or gruff—of the occupant of the office? The greater "miracle" is the one we have!

The trouble with Paul VI is, in part, that we know him mostly by photography and television—media that even in Holland often convey different impressions than physical presence. I have always been touched, as have many visitors to the Eternal City, by the warmth of the papal audience of Paul VI. There is a charm in the man. Peter Nichols in his book, *The Politics of the Vatican,* has given, it seems to me, a more just impression of Paul VI:

> Though Paul in Italy is accounted a rather unremarkable speaker, he is, in fact, superior as a public figure to the statesmen of the contemporary world in the impression he can convey of real moral sincerity combined with a highly professional knowledge of affairs. His occasional naivete can make him more attractive, for it shows him to be touchingly human: a trait that does not readily emerge from the formal transactions of his office.

But the point is that any pope will be human.

And even if he is the incarnation of spiritual liberty, humility, intelligence, wit and eloquence, we will still find it difficult to believe. Many people believe a non-Italian Pope is the answer. Yet, that non-Italian Pope will have to come from somewhere and some Spaniard, or African, or Columbian or American will not like him.

Furthermore, as Nichols also noted, "John XXIII showed that the best 'foreign' Pope was a real Italian." In other words, for someone, the Pope will always be either too anxious or too fat, too deceptive or too jolly, too easy-going or too thin, too simple or too intelligent, too efficient or too boorish, too short or too tall. Does our faith depend upon these questions of efficiency and likeability that a man may have? If so, I, for one, can no longer believe. There are all sorts of things I do not like about the way the Church is run. They should be improved. But do we lose our faith over them? Do we get too serious about them? The greater miracle is always that God did *not* establish a Church run by angels. Some modern theologians, I know, would say that the reason for this is that angels do not exist. I prefer to believe that "the foolishness of God is wiser than men," that even if a dead man appeared from Abraham's bosom, we would still call for "a second and fuller conference."

Not Bound to Stay After Litanies

In reading William Cobbett's marvelous *Rural Rides* once, I came across the entry he made for

August 31, 1826, when he was entering the Cathedral at Salisbury at seven in the morning. I have since seen Salisbury, and I have always been moved by John Constable's various paintings of it. So the scene is easy to reconstruct. Cobbett, in his usual crotchety mood, entered this "most magnificent and beautiful cathedral" to find a parson, four men, and five ladies.

Cobbett's principal preoccupation was what the founders of the Cathedral would say if they, like Lazarus, could rise from the dead to see what happened to their endowments. But giving us a lesson in good English moral theology, he did not stay long in church: "I joined the congregation until they came to the litanies; and then, being monstrously hungry, I did not think myself bound to stay any longer."

When we think of the problems of authority and the faith today, we wonder whether future generations will look upon ours as Cobbett looked at Salisbury: "For my part, I could not look up at the spire and the whole of the church at Salisbury, without feeling that we lived in degenerate times. Such a thing never could be built now. We feel that as we look at the building. It really does appear that if our forefathers had not made these buildings, we should have forgotten before now what the Christian religion was!" Are the present authority forms we so much seek to change merely things, like Salisbury Cathedral, that "never could be built now?" If the Rock of Peter, like unleavened bread, is a form to be changed into hamburger, we need not stay after the litanies. And today we are always hungry.

Myths and Itching Ears

I believe in the ironies suggested by Paul to Timothy and the Corinthians, namely, that there is at work in the foolishness of God a human wisdom that is wiser than men. "The time is coming when people will not endure sound teaching, but having itching ears, they will accumulate for themselves teachers to suit their own likings, and will turn away from listening to the truth and wander into myths." (2 *Tim.* 4:4)

Now I take it that this is not meant to excuse inefficiency and corruption in high places, though it does help to understand them. Yet the meaning of Christianity is that the human intelligence, however adequate it may be, has a genius for opposing God's plan for human salvation so that there is always possible, even likely, a conflict between the wise of a given generation and the very human institutions that were established around Peter and the Apostles. "There is in it (history,)" Christopher Dawson has reminded us, "always a mysterious and inexplicable element, due not only to the influence of chance or the initiative of the individual genius, but also to the creative power of spiritual forces." This creative power is in the direction of preventing the intellectual myths of a generation from obscuring the truths and life that God has given to men. There is, in other words, an instinct in the Church that seems to know when mankind is threatened. Moreover, it is, more often than not, the events of history themselves that begin to clarify what is at stake.

If we look at the broader world today, what is

most striking is that authority is a universal problem. Its uncertainty in the West seems to threaten the very continuity of that society. In the East, the names of the Soviet leaders and the Chinese ones too suggest that iron, powerful, unyielding strength lies behind authority that is not chosen. We have, furthermore, a world-wide climate of opinion that tells us that having children is a threat to mankind, that sex will become more fun if it is liberated from its dependence on fertility.

What is remarkable to me is that if we ask who it is that consistently seems to feel threats to the human race on these issues that are so vital to the men who actually exist, I find—much to my surprise, I confess—that *it is the papacy that seems to be on the side of man in spite of all the anxiety, and the improbability of the human element in the Church.*

My contention is that we have in the papacy of the Sixth Paul a force which retains the centrality of the human person and all the dire and happy issues of our times. Christianity is about life a life that comes from God and returns to him. The Pope has followed, explained and defended this life: in human intelligence, in religious and priestly vocations, in his struggles for peace, as it is born among us and as it grows and develops. Is life worth living? Paul's answer to the age-old question is a resounding "Yes!"

The Pope's Mind

2

Paul is not merely a pastoral Pope but a highly intellectual one. He is familiar with the terminology and tendencies both of classical and modern thought. He is the first Pope to make widespread use of quotations and reflections from non-papal, biblical and patristic authors. These are reflections of a Pope who is concerned not merely about the intellectual origins of faith problems but with the very nature of intelligence itself.

Jean Guitton, in his interesting but difficult to evaluate book *Dialogues avec Paul VI* has endeavored to emphasize that in this Pope, the Church in fact has one of its most intellectual pontiffs in its history.[1] That we do not instinctively realize this is something of a pity. Part of the reason (at least for the English language public), is that the vast corpus of his writings and speeches, both before and after his elevation to the papacy, are only partially translated and this in journals or books not at all easy to come by. Very few, if any, of our universities or seminaries make any sort of systematic effort to study what he has accomplished. I venture to say that there are few private study groups or scholars working or reflecting on Paul.

Anyone who begins to read Paul carefully will immediately be struck by the breadth and pertinence of his general literary and scientific, as well as theological and biblical, knowledge. After discovering again and again even for my own skeptical mind that Paul does understand most of the major points at issue within the modern mentality, I have become more wary about ignoring what he has to say. His intelligence is very active and wide-ranging. It is difficult to avoid the impression that he is in full control of what he wants to make known to those willing to listen. I do not say this out of any spirit of adulation or uncritical enthusiasm. It is a natural and rational reflection of one human person coming in contact with another obviously quite alert, rational, and aware man who knows what is generally happening in the often obscure realms of intelligence.

The first way I should like to particularize the papacy as it has been lived by this Pope, is from the viewpoint of his intelligence, from his stress on science and knowledge, from his acute awareness of the need the Church constantly has of intellect. One of the abiding aspects of Catholicism, of course, has been historically its persistent stress on reason and knowledge within the faith. *Credo ut intelligam.* Further, there has been a consistent effort to recognize the wide range of scientific disciplines and knowledges within this tradition. If God be intelligent in some vast analogous sense, we cannot and must not expect human intelligence to be narrow or constrained in the pursuit of ultimate truth.

A rather negative characteristic of Catholic thought and intelligence, one stemming from the same concern for truth, has been obvious too. This has been the awareness and definition of error. Not all things are equally true and indistinguishable from one another. So a basic, even for many a disturbing part of the tradition of Catholic intelligence, an aspect that seems to fall upon the papacy with particular urgency and force, is the effort to clarify and state what is not in fact true. There is, within Catholicism a certain profound research for the intellectual and spiritual roots of what opposes reason and faith, and why it is that such opposition so often comes across as a superior intelligence.

Paul VI has known rather accurately the kinds of objections that arise against Christianity and against each of its basic institutions and dogmas. In a sense, this is consoling. In another sense, it is unsettling since we should often like to believe our own doubts are original with us, something that is, alas, only rarely the case. In a series of General Audiences he gave on the Faith in 1967, Paul demonstrated his grasp of this negative and, for him, rather unpleasant but necessary aspect of his office. "It would be interesting to make a synthesis of the objections to the faith which characterize our era," he reflected.

> Especially we should note that many of these objections arise from the *forma mentis,* that is, from the very manner of using our faculties of knowledge to which we have been formed almost from our growth through schools, science, and the modern mentality. It would be equally interesting to ascertain which of the new difficulties—today terribly radical and placing all in question—come to be added to those of yesterday. Actually, in the world of thought, everything is doubted and so equally in religion. It would seem the spirit of modern man finds rest only in total negation, in the abandonment of all certitude, of all faith....
>
> As far as we are concerned, among the general and principle causes of our present difficulties and of eventual crises of faith, we would single out also the fact that modern

thought, even in certain sectors of Catholic teaching, has detached itself from what is called the *philosophia perennis,* that is, from the natural norm of human reason and also from the fact that we have rather a tendency to defy the magisterium of the Church.[2]

Such are not the words of a merely pastoral Pope but of a highly intellectual one, one familiar with the terminology and tendencies both of classical and modern thought, especially familiar (some would say too familiar), with currents of French thought. Paul, in any case, is the first Pope to make wise and widespread use of citations and reflections of non-papal, biblical, and patristic authors in his major works. These are reflections of a Pope who is concerned not merely about the intellectual origins of problems with the faith, but with the very nature of intelligence itself, with the very structure of the human mind.

Space

During the pontificate of Paul VI, undoubtedly the most striking event in the scientific world was the landing of men on the Moon and all that implied. This was an "event," a change in the condition of men on this planet which will effect the future of the human race in some as yet unfathomable manner. Space conquest was the result of a long history of the development of science and technology, a four or five hundred year old history that has long been a major issue between faith and knowledge. Moreover, both Pius XII and Paul VI himself have in recent decades especially been concerned about the implications of this scientific mentality in making man more or less human.

Interestingly enough, the Pope often refers to the Psalms and to Pascal when he deals with space. Pascal's infinite spaces that frighten, his idea that in thought man comprehends the universe are simultaneous reactions of Paul confronted with the vast projects of the cosmos. When Frank Borman visited him in 1969, the Pope began his talk to Borman with Psalm 18, "The heavens are telling the glory of God...." And this is a clue to the absolute realism with which the Christian faith confronts our knowledge of space and its meaning. "Today man's admiration of God's handiwork speaks with a new voice," he told the American astronaut. "Man's reaching out to unravel the mysteries of the universe reveals more and more the wonders of God's work and shows his glory."[3]

One of the striking things about the intelligence of Paul is its readiness to associate directly the basic truths of Christianity with this particular universe and man's unique place in it.

> (This space venture) ... will remind (man) of the staggering proportions of the universe as compared to our tiny size; it will encourage him to consider earthly life in more exact and communal terms; it will awaken in him the sense of the mystery of human life, its destiny and its relation to the Primary Being who has created the cosmos....
>
> Man's stature, compared to that of the cosmos, is at once immensely great and immensely small. The Christian mystery, which rests on man, makes obvious this double dimension of our being, and prepares our thinking process for the dizzy considerations of cosmic experience.[4]

Paul bears that instinctive philosophical realism that finds order in the cosmos confronted by the human mind made to know it in all its implications.

In 1973, on the occasion of the Fifth Centenary of the birth of Nicholas Copernicus, who stands at the very origins of modern astronomy, Paul VI wrote to Cardinal Stefan Wyszynski in Warsaw on the meaning of faith and scientific knowledge, a problem of the modern age. Paul's words are not untypical of the stubborn Christian view that faith and reason are related to each other—and that the pursuit of truth is its own value and reward because it reflects ultimate truth.

> It is an old and familiar question whether these two—faith and science—are divided from one another or should be kept separate as mutually opposed, or whether the one harmonizes and can cooperate with the other. It must be stated clearly and openly that there is no objective or irreconcilable disagreement between the truth accepted on faith and the truth acquired through reason. Any difference or discordances which may arise between these two must be attributed to the weakness inherent in human judgments.[5]

In this context there is a legitimacy and proper object to religious studies and truth so that "the field which is devoted to deeper investigation has its own laws and order, and enjoys a certain autonomy, in as much as it accords with the will of the Creator."[6] Scientific work, is mostly effort and plodding, and yet "there is great satisfaction and happiness even in this kind of hard work, for knowledge of truth produces its own joy."[7] This latter remark of Paul's is of more than passing significance since it serves to counter-balance the current tendency to relativize all intellectual activity so that its sole and exclusive justification is some social or ideological purpose, a view which is itself based on a denial of Christian metaphysics.

His reflections on space and its relation to faith

can also be seen in his remarks on the passing of the Comet Kohoutek early in 1974. These are especially pertinent, as they quite graphically connect the cosmos in which we live, the one that goes on about us without our having to set it in motion and which we scientifically investigate, with the very creation and redemption we Christians believe in. In a paradoxical way, there is a very unsymbolic, unabstract context to Christianity. On observing the Comet, Paul pondered out loud what he saw and what struck him, almost a poem.

> Once more we felt the sense of cosmic mystery! Limitless space, time without end, the setting of countless stars, the perfect, inexhaustible movement, the frighteningly profound silence, the phenomena of matter so thoroughly explored but, it can be said, still virtually unknown, the universe! And once more we were frightened (see Pascal, 205, 206), and stunned by the overwhelming, humbling contrast between its dimensions and ours, which are those of an atom, out of all proportion to the immensities stretching out on every side of existing reality.
>
> Then came the qualitative, logical reaction of the spirit: I think, I am. In fact, I dare say that I know everything, because this universe's page contains only one supreme passage, a name printed everywhere, an almighty, creating, ineffable name.... The word of God, Creator of the universe, landed personally on this fragment of the cosmos, our world; and he came to speak in human language among us! So there is no more fear, no more blindness! There is mystery still, but a mystery always open to our exploration and contemplation.
>
> Let us look at the sky again, brothers; let us look again at the universe, seeking in it a first, very rich natural revelation of God that is a framework for us of the second, supernatural revelation. This is the truth, a truth no longer menacing and frightening, but friendly and salvific.[8]

What is to be remarked in the Pope's varied reflections on contemplating space ventures and the men engaged in them is a profound sense of the intelligible compatibility with what is coming to be known and the essential revelation Christianity stands for. If the methods and sources of faith and science are in part different, still there is no doubt in his mind that there is one cosmos, one origin and destiny of all.

The Scientific Enterprise

When he comes to look more particularly at the work of scientists and their enterprise, Paul has consistently striven to uphold the autonomy and legitimacy of the various scientific disciplines. But he has wanted to place them all in a broader view which sees that scientific truth is itself part of the human condition in the most overarching sense, that there are priorities because man is mind and body, the personal locus, which makes our contact with the world and ourselves.

In the latter part of the last century and the early part of this one, the conflict between science and religion seemed to storm over the idea of evolution. This famous conflict is no longer so important, largely because the many exaggerated ideas of evolution to which the Church mainly objected have been dropped by the scientists themselves. Scientific biblical scholarship, too, has served to put the whole Christian perspectus in a more intelligible order.

About the only area in which this problem still arises for Christianity has to do with the reality and meaning of original sin, a doctrine which Paul VI,

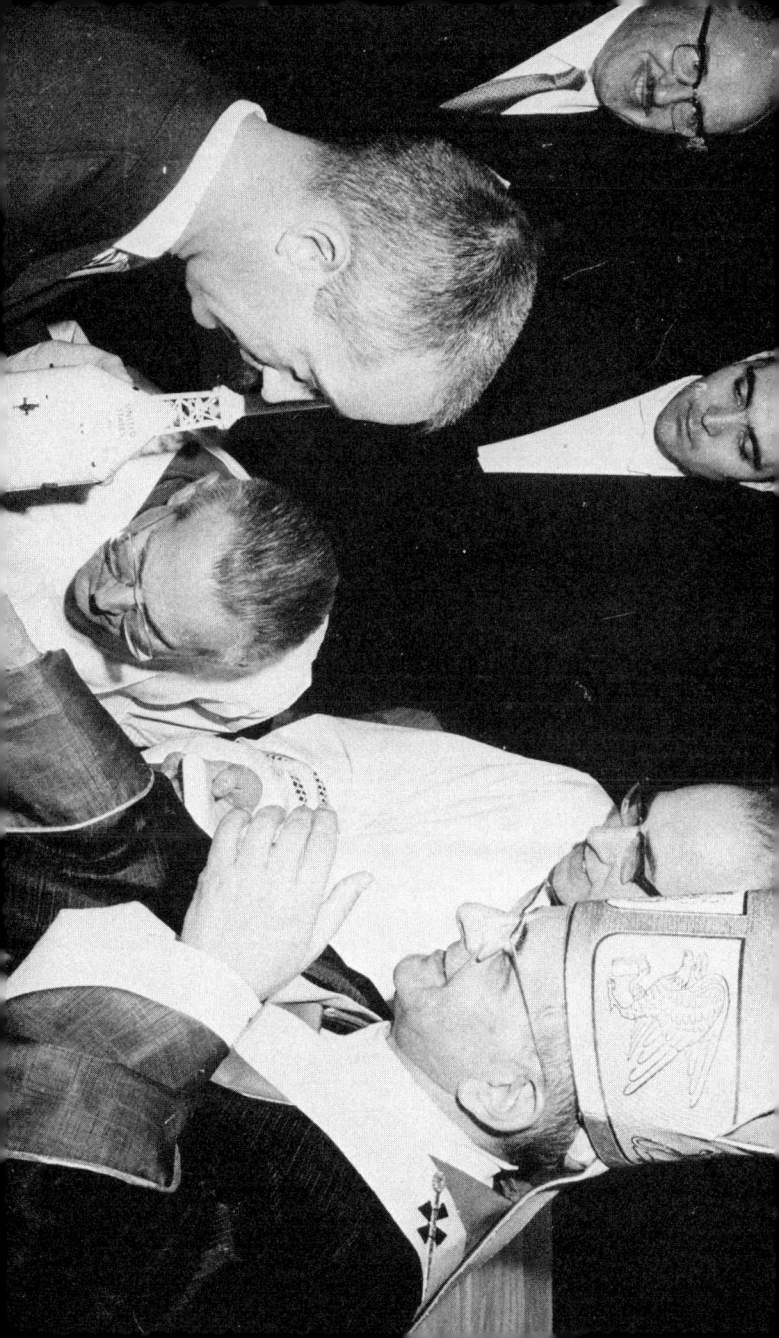

in an important address, reaffirmed and clarified in the context of the latest studies of evolution and theology. It is valuable in this regard not merely to note his firm grasp of the history of the problem itself, but the way he relates theology to science and research. The primary point he seems determined to make has to do with the uniqueness of each human person, a position that also lies at the basis of a good number of his essential positions, especially those arising in social philosophy, in population, in the place of man in the cosmos. The continued emphasis on original sin also challenges those popular utopian movements so prevalent since he first spoke, the ones that seek to proclaim that a perfect order is possible in the world.[9]

> The theory of evolution will not seem acceptable to you whenever it is not decisively in accord with the immediate creation of each and every human soul by God, and whenever it does not regard as decisively important for the fate of mankind the disobedience of Adam, the universal first parent. This disobedience must not be considered as not having made Adam lose the holiness and justice in which he had been constituted.[10]

This latter position looks to the very problem of the need for, and reality of, the kind of redemption men have received in Christ. The remarks take on further importance when we realize that a kind of secularized theory of original sin has subsequently emerged in the area of ecology and population theory to explain why man must be exclusively pessimistic of his fate—the opposite to the extreme from which evolutionary theory first set out.[11]

Paul has endeavored to clarify the classical Catholic view that original sin is indeed a reality that must be accounted for, but that it does not destroy the validity of human knowledge nor prevent man from acting for a good purpose. It does make this latter task difficult, subject both to evil and error, as ancient and modern history abidingly prove. This is why the Pope has been most sensitive to scientific theories when they touch, one way or another, the nature of man and society.

"No one claims that the Church should become a specialist in any particular field such as economics or sociology," he told the UN Advisory Committee on the Application of Science and Technology to Development. But this does not mean there are no moral or religious influences that might guide what development is for. "This common goal is a desire to come to the aid of our unfortunate brothers, to those millions of men who cannot eat well enough to satisfy their hunger.... For there are no genuine prospects of progress, balance and peace for mankind without the intervention of moral and religious facts."[12]

In awarding the Pius XI Medal for scientific research to Professor György Némethy, of Rockefeller University in New York, Paul was again concerned that scientists direct themselves in particular to those numerous areas of food and development where men need help most. And yet, he continued to the Pontifical Academy of Science, "The disinterested search for truth and the tireless pursuit of the secrets of the universe are, in fact, among the highest values, the most enthralling ideals, to which man can devote his life."[13] And Paul is constantly aware that a scientific search for truth must lead, almost in Augustinian fashion, to a higher wisdom.

> Nature, gradually mastered, reveals a mystery greater than itself. Here the scholar is invited to become a philosopher. Either at the beginning or at the end of the enigmas he encounters on his way and which he works to solve, he is led to recognize or at least to perceive the presence of a wisdom of another order, unlimited, transcending space and time, that explains the presence of these laws....[14]

The characteristic aspect of Paul's view of science carries forth this simultaneous awareness of the powers of the human intellect to know and to assimilate as well as to mark the dangers of the human will in the use of science, a danger that arises from a practical awareness of the tradition of original sin.

In a sense, the Catholic mind as exemplified by Paul's remarks to scientists simultaneously stresses truth, research, honesty, and the reality of abuses.

> If you (scientists) are, in a sense, more fully human beings than other men, it is because you have developed to a higher degree the noblest and most godlike capacity of man: his power of thought, his ability to 'become all things' (*fieri omnia,* says classical philosophy). This is a unique and incomparable privilege which the human mind enjoys. The rational creature has the power to conquer reality, to assimilate it within himself, to make it his own truth even while it still retains its potential to become the common good of all men....
>
> (Science must) be employed to serve the welfare of mankind.... God grant that its (the world's) leaders and rulers will find the strength and wisdom to reject the evil use of the science of destruction....[15]

Paul VI has firmly maintained and renewed the positive attitude of religion towards science while at the same time clearly refusing to grant science an authority that would contradict man's place and purpose in the cosmos and in human redemption as it has been handed down through Christianity.

Universities

The history of relations between the Church and universities is a long and close one. In modern times, various theories of nationalism have worked against the founding or prospering of specifically Catholic universities in most parts of the world. In too many places, they are simply forbidden by force, in others merely tolerated. Almost never, except in Holland and Belgium, are they given anywhere near the adequate financial support they need. Usually, Catholic universities require strong private efforts if they are to exist at all.

Paul VI is under no illusion about the importance of having at least some Catholic universities that can adequately represent intelligence in both the modern world and in the Church itself. University culture is itself often so much a product of ideology or anti-religious mentality that any really "Catholic" intellectual development is rare unless there be universities under the sponsorship of Catholics themselves. In 1975, he remarked to the Presidents of Jesuit universities, "Culture seems, in fact, to be in rebellion, as it were, against man himself, even though he is its creator and promoter."[16] He was convinced that some universities were even playing down their specifically Catholic aspect so that many of the laity do not see how some universities are still Catholic, yet even non-Catholics

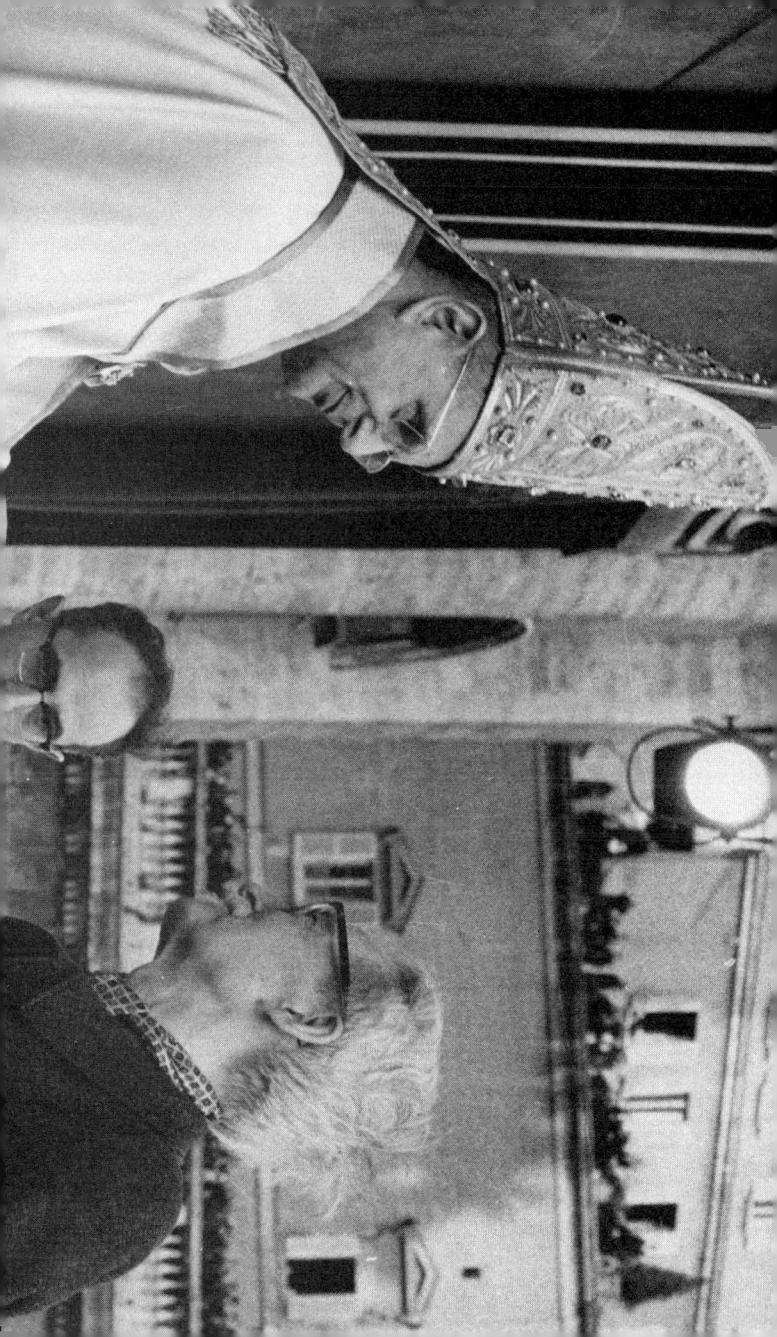

expect Catholic universities to know what the faith holds and teaches in the realm of intelligence.[17]

In 1971, the Pope wrote to René Maheu, Director General of UNESCO, that "it is not enough to give people a taste for knowledge and tools of power. We must also give them reasons for living."[18] Paul has ever shown a lively sense of the responsibility of man for his knowledge and heritage and for his resolving problems that arise because of great human diversity.[19] Yet he has not allowed his appreciation for the educated world as a whole to diminish his insistence on the specifically Catholic university. "The specific testimony expected of a Catholic university," he told representatives of world Catholic universities,

> ... is to show concretely that intelligence is never diminished, but on the contrary stimulated and strengthened by that inner source of deep understanding which is the Word of God, and by the hierarchy of values derived from it.... In its unique way, the Catholic university contributes to manifesting the superiority of the spirit, which can never under pain of being lost, agree to put itself at the service of anything other than the search for truth.[20]

And to the students of the Gregorian University in Rome, he insisted that "what is needed is a spirit of faith. An atmosphere of faith must invisibly but firmly guide every personal and collective effort and all free, historical and scientific research.... The decisive element is a religious view of the world, a *weltanschauung* inspired by the Catholic faith."[21] Even in this latter, more specialized, kind of university, we can see Paul's almost instinctive assumption that intelligence and faith necessarily belong together, freely and honestly, even for the sake of intelligence.

Conclusion: Newman and Aquinas

Jean Guitton has a fascinating passage in his reflections on the esteem Paul VI had for John Henry Newman.22 The Pope has shown a great familiarity with Newman. "Like Augustine, Newman knew what it costs in suffering to know the full truth," he wrote to a Newman Seminar in Switzerland. "He recalls to our mind that the search for the truth is an irresistible need of the human spirit...."23 He has recalled Newman's emphasis on conscience and on the development of dogma, especially pertinent topics during Vatican II over which he mainly presided.

> Newman's profound attachment to the Church is on a par with a demanding respect for the incommunicable dignity of the human person, for the unique and irreplaceable character of the person's vocation and his immediate responsibility before God. He knew how to glorify conscience....24

But what impressed him most about Newman, especially in the *Grammar of Assent,* was its insistence that subjective opinion was never enough but certitude needed to be "rooted in a reasoned conviction which may well rely on inner experience, but rests first of all on an objective revelation."25 Such is not a bad summary of the context in which Paul felt the discussion on religious liberty during the Council should be placed.

Like all modern Popes, when they return to the subject of intelligence in the Church, Paul again insists on starting with Aquinas. This is no narrow restriction or denial of the value of other philosophies, but it is a preference, an insistence that in Aquinas there is a method and an insight that continues to serve the human mind well. On the Seventh Centenary of the Death of Aquinas, Paul, in a long essay, wrote of him:

> He (Aquinas) held that the values and institutions of the world possess a relative autonomy, even while he uncompromisingly maintained the transcendent power and superiority of the ultimate goal to which all things earthly are ordered and subordinated: the Kingdom of God, which is the place of man's salvation and the basis of his freedom and dignity.[26]

Against both naturalism and fideism, Paul pointed out, stands the great Thomist principle:

> Grace does not diminish nature but brings it to fulfillment, while nature is subordinate to grace, reason to faith, and human love to divine charity. God's grace, which is the source of eternal life, presupposes and enlivens with new energies the whole complex of powers and faculties—existence (esse), intelligence, and love—through which the vital forces of nature are brought into play.[27]

There can be a real philosophy of being and a theology of Divine Being since Thomism is concerned first and foremost with the objective order.[28]

As Paul VI has assumed in all his discussions of intelligence, the mind can know what is true. There is a real confidence in its relation to the world, a real perception of order.[29] It is out of such a system that men can think intelligently of God.[30] Of course, he is quite aware that all philosophies and intellectual systems are not compatible with the faith on every score.

> At times, the basic principles governing a philosophy or a scientific position cannot be harmonized with religious faith due to an underlying monism or a denial of transcendental reality or subjectivism or agnosticism.
>
> It is regrettable indeed that many doctrines and systems

> of our day are thoroughly unreconcilable with Christian faith
> and theology. But here again St. Thomas comes to our aid,
> by showing us how particular elements in these systems can
> be used in the ongoing development and completion of
> Christian teaching, or at least how these systems can stimulate
> us to reflect on points earlier ignored or inadequately explained.[31]

There is here reaffirmed in the Sixth Paul both the openness of all Catholic thought to what men in fact hold and a critical recognition of a judgment, an evaluation of it, all in the light of a reason and a faith actively alert to what is true.

When we begin to look at this papacy of Paul VI in particular, I think, we first are struck by the importance of a Christian intellectual life that runs through all that he writes and speaks of. He has known and respected many of the acknowledged Catholic intellectuals of this century—a Maritain, a Gilson, a Guardini. Perhaps, it is true, a Pope cannot strictly speaking be an "intellectual." He must know so much more. He must rule and administer and care for the whole scope of human life that intellectuals historically are not concerned with. Still, as I shall constantly suggest, in each area of the religious life of modern Catholicism, Paul has shown an awareness, an alertness to the kind of intelligence that lies beyond or within external appearances.

Even more than Pius XII, who seems most like Paul of the recent Popes, the Pope has been alert to the intellectual problems that precede and accompany each aspect of the faith. He has insisted on knowing and stating fairly what the problems and objections are. He treats modern thinkers, poets, dramatists, novelists with sympathy. He cites them often. Moreover, he has displayed a talent for speaking of very profound religious or philosophical problems in a very simple way to audiences of every type of persons. As I suggested in the previous chapter, the presence and force of Paul VI in his person is quite remarkable, nowhere more so than when he speaks of intellectual problems and issues.

I should like to quote what he told a General Audience in 1968, in an address unfortunately difficult to find in English:

> There are many people today, even thinkers, especially the young, who fear that the idea of God becomes obscure and dissolves itself under the pressure of the new mentality born of scientific contact with the world, by the sentiment of force and liberty which man seems to try when we no longer feel ourselves subject to absolute transcendence. But that crisis can be resolved by means of a continual purification of the very idea of God and his worship, an idea always to be in progress, always necessary, always fecund, always living.... [32]

Paul never lets us forget that there is in fact something to be said of God, something that makes sense and that needs saying.

Christians have been used to the notion that philosophers can easily reduce themselves to foolishness by the proud use of their own rational faculties. (1 *Corinthians*, 1, 18 ff.; 2 *Timothy*, 1, 20 ff.) What is for many the most disconcerting (and for others the most refreshing) thing about the Sixth Paul is that, in those areas where he has been considered by many to be the most foolish, he has demonstrated a clear, consistent, even uncanny intelligence.

Who Is The Priest?

3

The Pope's major effort has been directed toward the priesthood, its problems and hopes, its meaning and its mystery. He seems to sense that attacks on the priesthood, or proposals that offer major and radical alterations in it, are part of a broader assault on the very possibility and meaning of Christianity in the world.

If we were to judge the Pope by a content analysis of his large corpus of writings and speeches, we would have to acknowledge the frequency with which he returns to the problems and meaning of the priesthood, vocation, and religious life in the Church. Especially the priesthood. It seems fair to say that these topics are the ones that most often have been discussed and can be rightly assumed to be the ones closest to his thoughts, concerns, and prayers. His emphasis on the priesthood and religious life does not seem to be judged by Paul to be some kind of neglect of the world or the laity but precisely the way that the Church's reality to the broader spheres and to all the members of the Church can be made real and vital.

Not only does he show a special awareness of his own priesthood, vocation, and life, but he seems to insist that the conditions of the priesthood, vocation, and religious life are major signs of the health or lack of it in the spiritual life of the Church.1 Religious and priestly life is what connects more closely the Church and its varied members, the People of God, with themselves as well as with the world, in the structure of salvation men have been given.

Since he was elected, Paul VI has managed to speak or write several times each year on some major aspect of religious and priestly life, including the meaning of the episcopacy and of the various religious families within the Church. He has been severest with the Jesuits, gentlest with the religious orders of women. All in all, he has managed to state the major anxieties that bother priests, religious, and bishops while clearly stating what he considers to be the abiding essence of these vocations within Christian tradition and structure which he insists it is his obligation to uphold.

Difficulties

The major effort of Paul VI has certainly been directed toward the priesthood, its problems and hopes, its meaning and mystery. He seems to sense that the attacks on the priesthood, the proposals that offer major and radical alterations in it, are not merely isolated shots but part of a broader perspective which has to do with the very possibility and meaning of Christianity in the world. Paul has a sensitive feeling for the modern priest who suddenly seems to find himself in a world no longer able to understand him, one indeed hostile to his very validity. He is able to state the various objections against the priesthood better than any one. If he disagrees with them, it is not because he does not know the arguments. He is too much an intellectual not to appreciate their full force and their origins and long range consequences. He is too much a Pope not to sense something deeper at issue whenever fundamental objections to the priesthood or basic alterations in its form are proposed.

The Pope holds that the major causes behind the unease with the priesthood are not merely those that come from newer customs but arise from theories of the Church, or society, or human nature which do not flow from the basic Catholic tradition, theories that see only political action, or psychological criterion, or sociological function or profession as important. The question is

> ... the so-called identity of the priest. Who is he? Who is the priest? Is there really a priest in the Christian religion? And if there is a minister of the Gospel, what role should he assume?
>
> All the temptations of the early Protestant controversy are being revived. And perhaps—this is a mystery, but not fantasy —even deeper temptations springing from a preternatural source have come to life: temptations of doubt, not as a method of research, but as a disheartened response proceeding from ungrasped truth and from uncertainty to the point of blindness.... These temptations have penetrated to the very center of the priest's inner conscience, so as to disturb his blessed inner certitude about his role in the Church: 'Thou art a priest forever.' In place of this a nagging question has been substituted, 'Who am I?'[2]

In 1971, he asked a General Audience, "What do you think of the priest?"[3] Paul is not ready to lay the total blame for problems on the heart of the priest himself. Indeed, he has consistently seen the priesthood and vocations to it in the larger scope of the religious health of the Church, especially the Christian family and community.[4] If the priest is to support, he also needs support. Paul expects priests to be able to rely on the broader Church.

The image of the priest in modern literature is a fascinating one for him who is quite alert to these literary images. He finds the priest such an interesting figure because of what is expected of him. Paradoxically, the many faults of priests are witnesses to their very vocation which somehow everyone recognizes and is the reason why literature can be so taken with priests who are full of faults. "But why do the faults of priests provoke so much reaction and criticism, so much readiness to generalize and condemn them?... Because we would always like to find perfection in the priest. Is not the priest the man of God, His representative and minister?"[5]

The Holy Father does not suggest that we ought to have a perfectly faultless priesthood, something quite contrary to the Christian inspiration, but he does draw from this a very realistic and sensible recognition of the way priestly life needs to be formed and fostered, one with a real awareness of the fallen human nature which priests also bear. This means prayer, asceticism, discipline, obedience—all those annoying realities which we would all prefer to ignore.

The Pope also recognizes that the priesthood contains an element of strangeness or unintelligibility. It is not an office or a position that arises out of a rational analysis of community or its organization so that it is not a "right" to which humans are called on account of their own nature. Priests, in fact,

> suffer because of the frequently biased way in which certain facts of priestly life are interpreted and unjustly generalized. Therefore, we ask priests to remember that the situation of every Christian, and particularly of every priest, will always be a paradoxical and incomprehensible one to those who have no faith.[6]

This means that the priesthood must be understood within the context of a divinely established hierarchy, an organized Church in which it is not given even to the Pope or to the episcopacy to change, but rather to explain and make alive.

Pope and Priests

In a real sense, it is not possible to understand Paul VI without realizing his grasp of his office as Pope and of his own priesthood, for it is in this capacity that he often speaks of the nature of the priesthood. When he was in Bogota in 1968 visiting a poor parish, he gave one of his most engaging descriptions of how he views himself.

> And who am I? You know: I am a man, just like you, a simple and needy person—in need of the mercy of God and of your prayers, because I have been given charge, without merit or choice on my part, of representing the Lord Jesus. I am the Successor of St. Peter, the Apostle to whom the Lord gave the keys, that is, the powers of directing and sanctifying the Church, and of guiding all the faithful toward their salvation in paradise. I am the Pope, which means the father of all; I come to you therefore in the name of the Lord, and I wish that when you look at me, you would have your thoughts not on my humble person, but on Him, on Jesus, who is present in my ministry.[7]

These are remarkable words. Indeed, it is difficult not to like someone who could speak so simply of what is one of the most difficult and enigmatic positions in the world. Yet, they also reveal something of Paul's approach to the priesthood: it falls primarily within the structure of Christ's mission, in the Church, so that its nature is not something concocted by human group or organizational dynamics. Something of his attitude can be seen if we return to the discourse he gave to priests at the end of the Year of Faith (1968):

> To all priests, then, we say: never doubt your ministerial priesthood, for it is not a commonplace office or service to be exercised for the ecclesial community, but a service which participates in a very special manner, through the Sacrament of Orders and with an indelible character, in the power of the priesthood of Christ.[8]

The sacred, apostolic, ascetic, and ecclesial aspects of the priesthood are all based upon the Sacrament that is given and to which it is the Church's obligation to be faithful.

Paul never seems to doubt that many are in fact called to the priesthood—and he insists that it is a "call," something not primarily of human origin. No one is "worthy" of the ministerial priesthood. He feels that the various proposals for abolishing celibacy or making the life of the priest more like that of the laity in various ways are in fact counter-productive. If the priesthood becomes just another job, with no sacrifice demanded, no one would see anything challenging or divine about it.[9]

> The priest is not simply a presbyter presiding over the community on religious occasions. He is truly the indispensable

> and exclusive minister of official worship performed in the person of Christ and at the same time in the name of the people. He is the man of prayer, the only one who brings about the Eucharistic sacrifice, the one who gives life to dead souls, the dispenser of grace, the man of blessing.[10]

The major burden of all Paul's reflections on the priesthood is to keep clearly the divine origin of this office and the supernatural aspect of the Church and its destiny before the eyes of the priests and all Christians.

Fundamentally, the priesthood exists among men for a divine purpose and it is that which priests essentially represent. Paul's last answer is quite straightforward:

> Do not be afraid of the problematic atmosphere surrounding the priesthood.... The novelty of tendentious biblical studies, the authoritative air of sociological phenomena studied in statistical terms, the stress laid on psychological and moral phenomena might seek to turn the crisis into a death dealing blow to the priesthood....
>
> The authentic nature of the priesthood holds its own... even in the face of the religious modern world. This world, precisely because it is what it is and because it has made such great strides in exploring and conquering things accessible to our experience, is growing ever more aware of the mystery of the surrounding universe and the illusory nature of our self-sufficiency. It is exposed to the danger of being enslaved and desiccated by its own progress; and it is making a desperate effort to find ultimate truth and the life that does not perish. In a world like ours, the need for someone who carries out a mission of transcendent truth, supernaturally motivated goodness and eschatological salvation is not annulled; it is needed.[11]

The Bishops

Paul VI speaks to bishops and of their office in

a rather different style and manner than he does to priests and seminarians. He knows their office and his are united in the governance of the Church. In Bogota, he reminded the Assembly of Latin American Bishops that the first principle of Christian personalism applied to them too: "Surely no one would deny that we bishops, called to practice perfection and to sanctify others, have an immanent and permanent obligation to seek our own perfection and sanctification."[12] He simply seems to assume that bishops are the successors of the Apostles and have an authority ultimately originating in the very heart of the Godhead. Paul does not hesitate to see the episcopacy as from God. In 1972, when he elevated nineteen new bishops, he told them:

> The Church, founded on the Apostles, comes from an eternal plan of God the Father, who through the ancient covenant chose His people, the heir to the messianic promises, and gathered it together through the sacrifice of His only Son through the rite of the new covenant. The apostolic succession is the guarantee of that unity for which Christ died and rose again. The bishops preside over local Churches which, although separate in time and space, never cease to be the one People of God, just as God is one—God who calls and sanctifies them.[13]

Paul is also quite aware of the current objections to the episcopacy and of its own problems.

> We are aware that some have recently ventured to place the charismatic and the hierarchical Church in opposition, as though it were a matter of two distinct, indeed contrasting and opposed bodies. On the contrary, in this pastoral power, charism and authority are one and the same thing. We receive the Holy Spirit who manifests himself in the episcopal mission through the vital combination of teaching, ... ministry, ... and governing. ... These are all powers of the bishop and

also gifts of the Spirit....

From the one Triune God comes the one Church, for which the bishops have primary responsibility, sharing as they do both charismatic gifts and hierarchical offices in a unique way.[14]

One has to remark of Paul VI in such a context that he is neither afraid to state who the bishops are nor how he disagrees with criticism of their special place in the Church. The background of his firmness, I think, is his conception of the hierarchy's essential task:

Now can we suppose that the hierarchy is free to teach what it likes in the religious field, or to teach according to the whim of certain doctrinal—or rather antidoctrinal currents of modern opinion? No, it is not. We must remember that the episcopate is invested with a primary duty, that of testimony—the scrupulously faithful transmission of Christ's original message, of the body of truths He revealed and entrusted to the Apostles with regard to salvation.[15]

This sense of fidelity to what he has received, what the bishops along with himself are bound to pass on, is what is most characteristic of Paul VI. When he speaks of fidelity, as he often does, it is this sense that the faith is not something men form for themselves, but something they have been given and are to hand on.[16]

Yet, he acknowledges that the bishop, who should be a Good Shepherd also, "...is by no means in the serene, arcadian state which that title seems to assure him." In lines reminiscent of Solzhenitsyn, Paul sets forth why he holds that a modern bishop must also be a brave man.

Tell me, is it easy to be a bishop today? We mean a bishop who guides his flock, setting it on the right path; not one who reduces his duty to following the flock wanderings in

> accordance with which way the wind is blowing? We mean the vigilant bishop—teacher, educator, rector, sanctifier.... We are speaking of the bishop who considers and knows the world in its aggressive process of secularization, which strips man not only of his outward vestiges of Christian morals, but also corrodes every remaining moral and religious certainty he possesses....
>
> Where do we find in the men of our time the sense of God, the firm distinction between good and evil?[17]

No doubt he seeks in his bishops the kind of men who can hand on the tradition even against theological and critical currents in the Church that do not seem to support either the hierarchy or the papacy. One of the unique elements of this era which Paul is aware of is certainly the tension and opposition the hierarchy finds in the Church from those historically established within it to support it.

On the Epiphany, 1969, while he was ordaining another group of bishops, Paul aptly warned them:

> Today, orthodoxy—that is, purity of doctrine—does not seem to have a primary place in the psychological outlook of Christians. Many things, many truths are placed in doubt. Freedom often claims primary right over the authentic patrimony of Catholic doctrine, not only in order to study fully the richness of this doctrine, to deepen it and to explain it, to modern man, but at times to subject it to the relativism in which profane thought experiments with its insecurity and seeks a new expression of doctrine.[18]

The modern bishop will be apt to find himself in a struggle within the Church over its very meaning. Paul insists that it is in the episcopacy, himself included, that the magisterium primarily resides. And so these men, whom Paul has more and more chosen from all over the world so that the episcopacy has never been more scattered among men, have a special position, chosen men who are not to serve without dignity or care. At another episcopal ordination in 1974, Paul remarked:

> Whatever the individual course of our lives that has brought us here... we can see in it a divine purpose, that has to do with each personality, a history reaching back, analogous to the one by which we have been given life; and it reveals to us a plan, an election, a love of Christ for each of us....
>
> Like the priest, but in a higher degree, the bishop does not exist for himself; he exists for the People of God. The episcopate is not a mere dignity for the one invested with it. It is a function, a ministry, a service for the Church.[19]

To a very great degree Paul sees the lives of his fellow bishops as providential, chosen by God in a very personal way. The dignity of the episcopacy and papal fellowship with the men in it are the backbone and structure of the Church's authority in Christ, a common task in which each supports the other.

Religious Life

If the hierarchy and the priesthood have a place in the Church more or less clearly defined and coming out of the founding structures from the Apostles, religious life for men and women is something more of a peculiarly Christian phenomenon whose spirit is rooted in Scriptures, to be sure, but whose full growth has needed inspiration and history to concretize. In his Encyclical *"Evangelica Testificatio,"* on Religious Life (1 November 1970), Paul again demonstrated his surprising grasp both of the difficulties presented to modern religious and their peculiar and essential place within the Church.

In the Roman Church, religious life has never been considered a state for everybody. There were diversities of spirit and office and vocation within the Christian Church, as St. Paul had insisted, so that this very diversity worked for the good of all and according to the needs of different types of people. Usually, religious life has been called a "pursuit of perfection" because its demands require special cares, rules, and objectives that ought not to be confused with the lives of priests or Christians who have their own kinds of holiness. The Church has always recognized that religious life and its demands can be dangerous to the greater good of ordinary lives of men and women if the goals and ideals of religious life be imposed on everyone.

Religious life is also considered to be "a doctrine of life that must be effectively lived."[20] The wide variety of religious life, the active and the contemplative, the special place of secular institutes, the various different spirits of the Franciscans, Dominicans, Benedictines, Jesuits, Sulpicians, and other religious families, constantly come under Paul's care and scrutiny. He is ever concerned both to situate religious life within the Church (how it relates to bishops, priests, and the laity), and to recognize the particular need the Holy See especially has of religious orders for special kinds of apostolates and needs.

In an address to Major Superiors of Men and

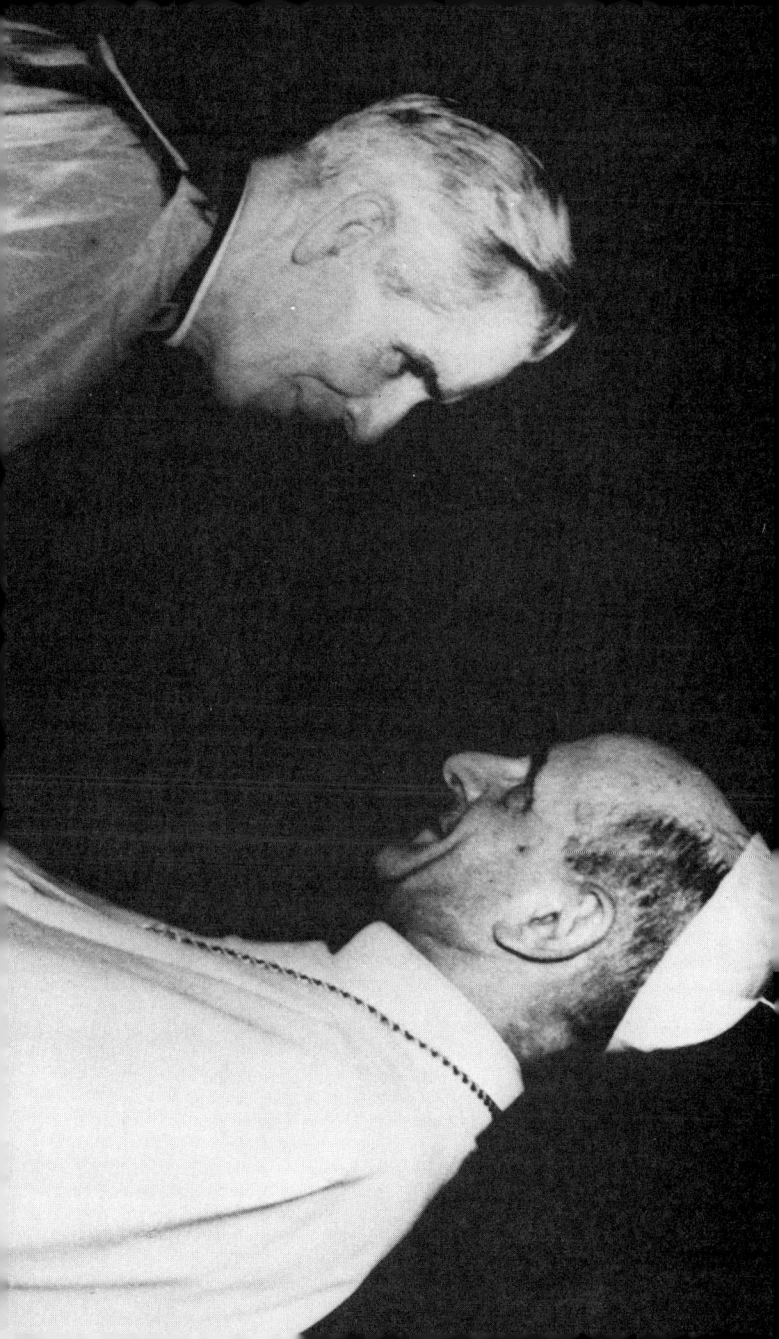

Women Religious (19 October 1972), Paul told them to be consistent and faithful to their own vocations. His sense of the basic value of religious life is noteworthy:

> Most Christians are called to affirm their faith and exercise their charity as laymen, with temporal responsibilities incumbent on them, and their witness essential.... But they all need precisely your faithfulness to your specific vocation as men and women religious.... In short, you must aim at evangelical perfection, so as to be permanently living signs of the transcendence of God's kingdom.[21]

Religious life is primarily viewed as a sign of what is more than the world, however much a religious person be devoted to active apostolates. Paul insists that religious show fidelity to the See of Peter and "a close, profound, cordial communion of sentiments and of actions with your bishops."[22] This, of course, flows directly from his concept of the essential structure of the Church. But at the same time, he sees that religious are essential to the Church for they represent its vocational freedom to seek more than is required, to witness to the truth that God alone is necessary.

To the First Assembly of Women Religious Superiors (7 March 1967), Paul VI affirmed:

> In a world that seeks to rid itself of absolute commands, that tends to regard all values as relative, the consecrated soul, focused unswervingly on God by its vows, is anchored in the absolute, as it were. Perhaps this, more than anything else, reveals the distinctively 'religious' character of your lives. While the religious may undertake external works of teaching, charitable activity or good works ... her activity derives its value from the interior charity that prompts this activity, from her union with God.[23]

The Pope has insisted on emphasizing the abiding need of the contemplative life in the Church, not only to remind us that lowliness and silence are also parts of the human reality, but to reveal that, in the Church, God above all is to be attended to. The noise, the travel, the media are everywhere, he told a General Chapter of Reformed Cistercians, so that "it is now more difficult to find quiet places of retreat where the soul might focus wholly on God and oneself."[24] The solitude of monastic life is itself a sign and remains important in the Church. The silence and the austerity of the monks are their way to pray for the Church and to remind all of the centrality of God.

Paul VI has frequently spoken to Franciscans and Dominicans over the years. Chesterton once said that for non-Catholics, Francis was the easiest saint to understand and love, while Dominic was the most difficult. The Pope continues to see an essential place for both. The Dominicans find themselves especially charged to retain that devotion to truth and knowledge with which the Church has come so often to associate herself.

> We have this to say: from the Sons of St. Dominic the Church very confidently expects fidelity to the doctrine of Aquinas, which must be further analyzed with regard to the questions posed by the world of today and in keeping with the full force and inner efficacy of that doctrine. Fidelity to St. Thomas is part of your special role in the Church.[25]

The Franciscans, on the other hand, naturally receive more emphasis on poverty. But Paul also goes further back to Francis' own emphasis on the Cross. In a sermon to Conventual Franciscans (12 July 1966), Paul reflected:

> What is the essential and typical aspect of (Franciscan)

> spirituality? Greccio and Alverna give you the answer: a humble and passionate love for Christ in his two principle mysteries, the Incarnation and the Redemption. This is what Francis lived, this is what he taught. And so it has been with his sons, right down to us.
>
> Isn't Franciscan piety Christocentric? Doesn't this spirituality start out from that contemplative gaze at Christ's humanity which begins with the simple and popular representation of the crib and His cross, and reaches the loftiest heights of mystical experience?[26]

Later, to a group of Third Order Franciscans, Paul wanted to emphasize the meaning of poverty and of the Cross, both of these elements in the faith need preservation and clarification. Poverty and the Cross in a way stand for the same realities, the insufficiency of this world to satisfy us, the fact that all is taken away in the end before we are to reach eternal life.

> ... Evangelical poverty means fixing our idea of life not on this earth, its riches, satisfactions, and pleasures, nor in what this world is and what it can give us, nor in the earthly kingdom, but in the Kingdom of Heaven, in the quest for and the possession of God, in freedom of the spirit from the bonds of the perpetual allurement of wealth, in the capacity to keep earthly goods within their proper sphere.[27]

The Cross is the "focal point" of Franciscan spiritual life. The Pope notes that besides the temptation of wealth today, there is also "the temptation to remove the Cross from the Gospel. People want an easy Christianity, a Christianity without sacrifice. They want a Christianity without duties, renunciation, superiors, or grief—in a word, without the Cross."[28] Of course, this is not Christianity.

In his public addresses to religious, Paul has probably been more stern with the Jesuits than with anyone else. This is both a compliment and a disappointment, conflicting sentiments which reveal a good deal about the character of Paul VI. To the 31st General Congregation (16 November 1966), Paul was quite blunt in wondering about the Society of Jesus' continued loyalty to the Holy See.

> Do you, sons of St. Ignatius and soldiers of the Society of Jesus, want to maintain today, tomorrow, and always that same attitude which you have always had toward the Catholic Church and the Holy See, from the very beginnings of your institute up to the present time? Normally, there would be absolutely no reason for asking such a question. But we cannot hide from you our amazement, and even our grief in some instances, on hearing certain reports and rumors regarding both your Society and other religious families.
>
> What strange and distorted influences could have caused doubts to arise in some sectors of your vast Society as to whether or not it should continue to be the same as your holy founder originally conceived it and as he so wisely and firmly established . . . ?
>
> Perhaps even some members of the Society have adopted the theory of an absolute historicism which states that all human things, because originating in time, are by time inexorably destroyed, as if Catholicism possessed no prerogative of permanent truth and unshakable stability—a prerogative in fact symbolized and founded on the firm rock of the Apostolic See itself.[29]

He was confident that such problems could be resolved. "The Church needs your help," he told the Jesuits. The ambivalent world, of two faces, "one representing the conspiring of all those who fight against the light and against grace; the other comprising the immense mass of the human race" calls out for aid and strength.[30]

At the 32nd General Congregation, in 1974, Paul

still confessed "a certain anxiety."[31] He reaffirmed the Jesuits' special nature as an apostolic and clerical order with special obedience to the papacy. He again asked, again bluntly:

> Are you inwardly convinced of the fundamental truths of the Catholic faith and morality as proposed by the Church's magisterium and is your outward profession of them sincere? Are you determined to cooperate in an unreserved and trustful way with the Supreme Pontiff? ... Sad occurrences such as make us wonder whether a man still really belongs to the Society are only too frequent. News of them reaches us from every side, especially from diocesan bishops. These occurrences are a source of harm to the clergy and other religious and to the Catholic laity as well.[32]

These reflections were the Pope's most critical ones, (along with his letter to the Dutch Bishops).[33] They show a certain character both of confidence in the Jesuits and of obligation to his office on the part of Paul when he feels something is wrong in the Church. The overall impression is positive, a reminder that the papacy and the episcopacy are conscious of their task and that even religious orders may have to be called to account at times. This critical attention of the papacy is the other side of how Paul views the teaching function of the Church and its abiding loyalty to the structure and foundations established in revelation through Christ.

Life - giving Pontiff

4

The value and worth of *Humanae Vitae* become more evident if we attempt to see it in the larger context of the trends of scientific development, of birth prevention and of genetic control which are used to justify actions against human sexuality. It becomes clear that serious life issues are here involved and that the document is in conformity with scientific development, and with the dignity of human sexuality which is really what is at stake.

Perhaps no papal document has caused more controversy and more anguish to the Holy See than the Encyclical on *Human Life*. Many purport to find it a fatal error on the part of the papacy. Some think it unscientific. Others accuse it of ignoring population growth. Still others find it an interference with private lives.

Paul VI has accepted and responded to all of this criticism. But interestingly enough, he has not changed his initial views and has insisted on the conformity of this document with the long-range good of man. He has insisted that the issue is precisely one of a defence both of family and of sex itself. Many of the practices which he foresaw would happen from a denial of the document's central thesis have in fact come about.

Must we agree with the harsh criticism and concede that he made an error, that the issue is not as serious or as central as he made it out to be? I should like to be a minority here and suggest that he did sense something very basic about the threat to human life and that his fundamental stand really serves to defend the dignity of the kind of human life we are given.

A few days after the publication of this most controversial encyclical on birth regulation and human life, I found myself being treated in the beautiful Monterey Peninsula Hospital in California for a rather uncomfortable head injury. When the considerate young medic on emergency duty learned that I generally teach in Rome during the scholastic year, he immediately launched into a detalied and highly impassioned attack upon the papal birth control views which seemed to him outlandish and unscientific.

At the time, I was really in no mood to participate in a debate on this rather loaded topic, but one random doctor's attitude certainly became typical of the utter incomprehension with which this well-publicised decision of the papacy was greeted in the public forum.

The acuteness of the problem became equally visible in other instances. Many emphasized the crisis of authority the document presented to the Church. Others claimed it would be ignored. A young Catholic housewife in great distress wondered on the morning of the encyclical's appearance just how it would be possible for her to seem anything but ridiculous in the eyes of non-Catholic friends, who certainly would find the document's proscriptions at variance with their own experience of birth prevention. In a letter to the *Oakland Tribune,* a University of California biology professor accused the Pope of being directly responsible for the death of millions of human beings as a result of his position (August 3, 1968).

In the years following this document, on the contrary, its denial has rather been responsible for the deaths of millions of fetuses. We are still, however, in great need of some acceptable approach that might make the Magisterium's conclusions seem at least comprehensible. Undoubtedly in judging the work of Paul VI, one's view of *this* document will often determine how one can accept the *whole corpus* of his work.

Before setting down the reasons why I think Humanae Vitae will eventually prove to have been spiritually and dogmatically necessary at this period in history, it might be well to state clearly the major intellectual difficulties it was thought to contain. There seem to have been four uncertain points: 1) the theological status of the document; 2) the problem of naturally infecund acts; 3) the relation existing among the various marital rights, and 4) the problem of the right of conscience in the public order.

1. Form

The theological form in which this pronouncement was issued was that of an encyclical. Since the Pope chose specifically not to issue a 'de fide' type statement according to the established norms of Vatican I, we must presume the theological possibility, at least, of some kind of reformability of the statement.

We cannot be absolutely sure this is not a statement like religious liberty in *Mirari Vos,* the vocational groups in *Quadragesimo Anno,* like some of the statements of the Magisterium on socialism and communism as later modified by John XXIII's distinction between theory and practice, or like usury or the necessity of the Papal States (all propositions that were later changed).

Moreover, as Bernard Cooke wrote at the time, "since Catholic theology has always taught that a grave obligation may never be imposed on the Christian conscience unless that obligation itself is absolutely certain, the Pope's encyclical has not decisively altered the situation of practical doubt."[1]

As the Pope, presumably, did have the option to close definitively the issue by a stronger and more solemn statement (though there is some problem with collegiality even here, perhaps), the fact that he did not do this necessarily signifies some theological doubt may still be present.[2] A Catholic cannot assent to this statement with the same firmness as he can, say, to the dogma of the Trinity or the Incarnation. This does not mean, however, the statement's denial, therefore, becomes certain, as many seem to suggest.

2. Natural Law

Some "natural law" problems are not clearly resolved by the papal statement. "Natural law" must be what it says it is, a naturally persuasive or at least non-contradictory argument, (though this does not deny Aquinas' view that some natural law statements are more difficult to know than others). The crucial point is this: How is it possible that naturally infecund acts of intercourse (which biologically are the vast majority of acts between spouses even supposing a marriage producing twenty children) can naturally remain "open to the transmission of life?" (N. 11)

Is this not some kind of contradiction? It may not be, of course, and the growing loss of respect for incipient human life hints that it is not, but it is not so obvious on first glance why not.[3] To cover this objection, Paul VI cited the famous passage in *Gaudium et Spes* (N. 24) which stated that a true contradiction cannot exist between divine laws pertaining to the transmission of life and those fostering authentic conjugal love.

Nevertheless, it is not absolutely apparent from the Pope's own argument how he proves this relationship between naturally infecund acts and the openness to life transmission. How can a naturally infecund act be said to be open to life when that is precisely what it is not in the real biological order upon which the encyclical itself so heavily relied?

Why naturally infecund acts become "serious matter" when engaged in with contraceptives seems difficult to comprehend if what is at issue is the importance of the transmission of life which does not in fact take place. This position remains all the more difficult to understand when rhythm is clearly accepted as legitimate precisely on the grounds that acts are known to be naturally infertile. Why controlled infertility in the context of having some children is wrong, is difficult to see on the basis of the arguments given.

3. Natural Rights

The most poignant difficulty that arises from the encyclical is that little hope or help seems to be given to those couples who might want indeed to live according to the Church's norms but who have unknown or sporadic cycles. All that is offered to these people seems to be the Church's sympathy even if sin has a hold over them, (N. 25), and the hope that science will eventually come to their aid (N. 27).

Gaudium et Spes (N. 50) had affirmed that the responsibility for the transmission of life—numbers of children and their conditions of education—was up to "the parents themselves and no one else should ultimately make this judgment in the sight of God." But the principle, *qui vult finem vult medium,* still holds true, so that those many couples who have no "legitimate means" seem to be placed in a position of being naturally required to live in a constant condition of heroic virtue.

St. Thomas warned against this as a matter of legal principle. And St. Paul clearly affirmed "do not refuse each other except by mutual consent, and then only for an agreed time, to leave yourselves free for prayer; then come together again in case Satan should take advantage of your weakness to tempt you." (1 *Corinthians* 7:5). This also seems to suggest the impracticality and special danger of requiring long-term abstinence. One wonders why this passage and its implications has been so neglected.

If rhythm is the only legitimate means of birth-control, if a couple is really responsible for the size and condition of its family and if the spouses are not to "refuse each other" except "for an agreed time," it would seem that the following consequence clearly follows: a) woman must have a "natural right" to a known, controllable, certain cycle so that b) the couple can practically achieve the ends proposed by *Gaudium et Spes* by c) the means legitimated by *Humanae Vitae*.

The unknowability or irregularity of the female cycle must be considered a "natural defect" analogous to bad eyesight or defective hearing, a defect requiring scientific medical corrective to make it what it is supposed to be. Medical measures —and research for them—to achieve this natural right are certainly legitimate, indeed mandatory. In fact, it would seem the Church's major effort should go into this area as much as into education, missionary activity or welfare.

Paul's Reaction

One of the strengths of Paul VI has been a very clear and vivid appreciation of any set of objections to any part of the faith. He has shown, an uncanny ability to state the position of an adversary better than the adversary. He knew that he would be beseiged with criticism and even ridicule for the document. But he has left little doubt why he felt the decision necessary—Christians posed serious moral questions and deserved to have an authoritative response. In many ways, too, time has demonstrated quite clearly that all of the alternatives to Paul's views themselves have serious problems connected with them, either of health or protection of life.

On 4 August 1968 the Pope observed that *Humanae Vitae* had produced both favorable and unfavorable reactions. It is revealing of his character, one of loyalty to his office and tradition and comprehension of the difficulties involved, to note how he conceived his duty in this matter:

> Our encyclical *Humanae Vitae* has caused many reactions. But as far as we recall, the Pope has never received so many spontaneous messages of gratitude and approval for the publication of a document as on this occasion.... We know, of course, that there are many who have not appreciated our teaching, and not a few have opposed it. We can, in a sense, understand their lack of comprehension and even their opposition. Our decision is not an easy one. It is not in line with a practice unfortunately widespread today which is regarded as convenient and, on the surface, helpful to family harmony and love.
>
> Once again we would remind you that the ruling we have reaffirmed is not our own. It originates from the very structure of life, love, and human dignity, and is thus derived from the law of God. It does not ignore the sociological and demographic conditions of our time. Contrary to what some seem to suppose, it is not in itself opposed to the rational limitation of births. It is not opposed to scientific research and therapeutic treatment, and still less to truly responsible parenthood. It does not even conflict with family peace and harmony. It is just a moral law—demanding and austere—which is still binding today. It forbids the use of means which are directed against procreation and which thus degrade the purity of love and the purpose of married life. The duty of our office and pastoral charity have led us to speak out.[4]

What persists in all Paul's reflections on this issue is the awareness of a direct threat against life, against love, against sex and marital life itself. In a sense, it is uncanny how just these issues have become more and more central in every modern society.

In a more lengthy address to a General Audience on 31 July 1968, Paul left no doubt about how much the problem had been studied, about his own view of his office, and his sympathy for any difficulties. "Many times we trembled before the dilemma of giving in easily to current opinions, or of making a decision that would be hard for modern society to accept, or that might be arbitrarily too burdensome for married life."[5]

He felt the issue was the dignity of marriage and the divine law which alone gives it its ultimate meaning. So the document has the full weight of the Magisterium even though there might be some technical discussion about whether it is "de fide." "We pondered the consequences of one decision and the other; and we had no doubts about our duty to set forth our decision in the terms expressed in the present encyclical."[6]

The Pope possesses a kind of earnest way of inviting fellow Christians to share his reasoning and his values. In spite of the way his views are often presented, he himself seems most straightforward in explaining the values he feels must govern the discussion.

> Another feeling that always guided us in our labors is that of charity, of pastoral sensitivity toward those who are called upon to integrate their individual personalities into conjugal and family life. We willingly followed the person-

alistic conception that was characteristic of the Council's teaching on conjugal society, thus giving love—which produces that society and nourishes it—the preeminent position that rightly belongs to it in a subjective evaluation of marriage. Then we accepted all the suggestions formulated within the bounds of what was licit, to facilitate observance of the norm which we reaffirmed. We wanted to add to the doctrinal explanation some practical directions of a pastoral nature.

We paid tribute to the role of scientists in pursuing their biological studies on birth, and in rightly applying therapeutic remedies and the moral law inherent in them. We recognized the responsibility and freedom of spouses as ministers of God's plan for human life, which is interpreted by the magisterium of the Church, for their own personal good and that of their children. And we stressed the lofty purpose running through the Church's teaching and practice: that of helping men, defending their dignity, understanding them and supporting them in their difficulties, training them to have a keen sense of responsibility, a strong and calm mastery over themselves, a courageous concept of the great and common duties of life and of the sacrifices inherent in practicing virtue and in building a fruitful and happy home.[7]

These kinds of reaction reveal a man totally conscious of his own duty, his comprehension of difficulties, and the nobility of what he proposes to men and women.

The Encyclical and the Future

With these problems connected with the papal document in mind along with Paul's own understanding of his views, let me now state why the encyclical seems both advisable and even prophetic in our time.

First, I am convinced that the problem of so-called "illicit birth-control means" is largely a temporary issue in its present form. It will sooner or later be resolved for *all* men in a form that will look pretty much like the Church's traditional teaching. The reason for this is clear, if surprising.

The actual pressure on science in this area is "naturally" (I use the term both deliberately and paradoxically) to produce a secure birth-control method which fulfills the substantial requirements of the papal norms. This is a most ironic result! But it strikes me that any alert reflection upon the actual history of contraception makes it evident that the pressure on science welling up spontaneously from the demands of the sexual community is to produce a secure, safe method of birth-control which allows *the natural act to be the natural act*.

All scientific progress in this area has in fact been in this direction anyhow because what man instinctively, that is, naturally prefers in his sexual relations is either the natural act itself, or, this lacking, something approximating it as closely as possible. In essence, everyone admits the natural superiority of the sexual act as it is received from nature. In other words, no one wants to use birth control-prevention means and in fact no one does, *except* when constrained by some other reason.

Birth control is in practice used only to prevent disease or birth when these motives are strong enough to overcome the natural desire not to interfere with the sexual act. All acts of contraception are taken against what the participants prefer with regard to the consummation of the act itself. Contraception means the limitation of the act is preferred by many to nothing. But it is *not* preferred to the act as it is found in nature where this is available.

The act as it is given by nature is always selected when the choice itself is given. And the ready acceptance of abortion as a contraceptive in the years since Paul first wrote, persuasively argues further that many people who are quite capable of using contraceptives, do not and prefer the natural act to them, so that unwanted conceptions are then aborted. Paul recognized that something like this latter would probably result.

If we list the known or proposed means of birth control according to their degree of deviation from natural sexual activity—i.e, infanticide, abortion, sterilization, contraceptive devices (IUD's condoms, jellies, diaphragms), the "pill," vaccine immunizations against the sperm, withdrawal, and rhythm—it is clear that the "reason" for the invention and development of each means was in some fundamental sense the unsatisfactory results with means that either attacked life, severed intact organs, interfered with the act of intercourse, or made it inconvenient.

And the history of the various "side-effects" to the various methods argues further that no alternative is really without its serious problems. In any case, the most "desired" means seems clearly, if this kind of approach is valid, to be *the one that allows and forms a normal female cycle that is both known, certain, and safe so that the natural act can be the natural act.*

Each new scientific improvement seems clearly designed to foster the human desire to allow the unimpeded natural act, which is the essence of the Pope's view. The condom and the diaphragm were means to avoid the necessity of abortion or the distaste for withdrawal. The "pill" was invented to avoid the inconvenience and interference of the condom and the diaphragm. The injections, sterilization, and the IUD were invented or perfected to avoid the side effects and sophistication of pill usage.

All of this seems to suggest that science is itself in fact headed in the traditional direction and that the invention of a secure rhythm system will not only prove immensely profitable but will be simply carrying to its logical conclusion a scientific progress that began with the rejection of infanticide as a legitimate means of birth control.

Science itself seems somehow to attest to the unacceptability of the present preventative means from the point of view of side-effects, of distaste and of effectiveness. We can be practically sure that all the present "means" will soon be little more than historic curiosities because mankind simply does not like them in its sexual activity.

This way of setting up the problem, moreover, makes it clear that human life is in some basic sense always involved in this discussion and that everyone must draw the line somewhere at the means of birth prevention in the name of man. Infanticide, as Will Herberg once vividly pointed out to a very startled protestant audience that refused even to consider his most valid point, is still the "best" means of birth control because it at least allows society to take a look to see whether what is being killed is defective or not. Abortion on the grounds that a fetus "might" be malformed or it "might" harm the mother is hardly so rational or even humane. The line must be drawn somewhere, then, in a continuum of life potential or actuality.

That some connection between abortion and contraception exists is strongly suggested by statistics in those countries where abortion laws are very liberal—most countries, unfortunately. Here the curious fact presents itself that illegal abortion still continues on a disturbingly large scale even among those who have all the contraceptive means available and knowledge about their usage. Contraceptive availability, contrary to common assumptions, *increases* the likelihood of abortions rather than reduces it! Indeed, we have seen abortion come to be looked upon simply as "back-up" contraception, a result that has probably not surprised Paul VI in the least.

All of this suggests that at the moment of intercourse many people, even though they have absolutely no moral scruple about the use of contraceptives, prefer not to use preventative means and that, once conception has taken place contrary to their desires, they have little hesitation in ridding themselves of what is conceived, as it was not desired in the first place. Not everyone who fails in contraceptive practice, of course, automatically resorts to abortion, but this question makes it evident that a connection between life and responsibility to the fact of intercourse does exist. And this is what Paul VI has argued all along.

The Not So Brave New World

However, even broader issues are at stake. To state this problem in its most extreme form: What is ultimately at issue is the very nature of hetero-sexuality itself. This will seem a bit preposterous to the average person, but any familiarity with proposals for genetic experimentation and control, or any analysis of the philosophical positions of homosexual and lesbian theory or the advocacy of any form of naturally "unreproductive" sex by population control groups, will soon reveal that it is precisely hetero-sexuality and its implications in love and the family that are at stake.

The question is this: Is man a certain kind of being who was established by "nature," so to speak, in a better form than man could produce himself? Can we improve on sexuality and still keep it? These two issues—genetic control of human life and the meaning of perversion—lie behind the defence of the natural act in marriage.

Too few people today are aware of the serious proposals being put forth in certain areas of the scientific community on this subject.[8] It is now possible at least theoretically to suggest—and it is being suggested and experimented with—that the hetero-sexual marital relationship, which does in fact produce real children from real parents, should be used only by a few for experimental purposes and that better genetic health could be produced by clonal generation rather than by sexual mating.

It is urged that eugenic selection of offspring should replace the present system where every man and woman has a right to form his and her own family, that the same genotype or only a few should form the whole of the human race, that everyone should be his own "twin," that children need no longer be conceived or developed in the womb of a woman—and perhaps even that all people should be of the same sex!

Implicit in many if not in all of these proposals is the notion that sexuality and its implications are the cause of the ruinous condition of the race and planet. Latent is the move to get rid of sex altogether. It is a subtle form of modern manicheanism which, I suspect, the Church senses better than most, a view that sex can be gotten rid of since it is not biologically necessary for the production and preservation of man, except perhaps as a kind of indifferent pastime that has no consequences in the empirical order.

Probably it is for this reason above all others that Paul keeps doggedly insisting that love, sex, and children must be kept together in one continuum. It is in defence of man as a naturally heterosexual being, whose dignity rests in large part upon the "naturalness" of man as he is received from nature, that makes this encyclical of Paul VI important. Man's natural system of reproduction is ultimately superior to any scientific or perverted alternative—the Magisterium has rightly taken its stand at this point.

This same conclusion is also implicit in the scriptural and traditional rejection of perversion as a normal form of human life, or even, as it is often argued more recently, a superior way of life for man. What fundamentally distinguishes "perversion"—that is, basically homosexuality, lesbianism, and bestiality—from the hetero-sexual relationship is its fundamental unrelatedness to the transmission of real human life and its subsequent sense of natural frustration.

In the broader context of these issues, together with some of the totalitarian implications of population theory which the encyclical rightly referred to, the papal document does mankind a basic service in suggesting that these are dangers in our intellectual and political environments that do strike at the very structure of man as we have known him. The issue is somehow, as most of the criticisms of the encyclical of Paul VI have suggested, the nature of human love and its "natural" exigencies.

If we look only to the narrow terms of the problem as somehow only pertinent to the pill or to contraceptives, we will miss the real threats to human life that abound in modern life and society, threats that are becoming clearer each day. These threats cannot be totally disassociated from the theory and practice of contraception or theories of population about the nature and potential of this planet.

Population fear, genetic control, and perversion do, furthermore, contain serious implications for the nature of man that we can no longer afford to ignore. Perhaps the biggest weakness of the encyclical was its failure to note these broader problems and their relation to the nature of human life. But there is little doubt that Paul VI suspected that such a broader scale was in fact present in the issue of human life.

Furthermore, as in the famous German Supreme Court case in Karlsruhe on abortion, he did not want either to forget his experience with totalitarianism. Millions and millions of our kind *are* being killed in abortions all over the world. Paul VI has persistently wanted to let the world know that this manifests one of the greatest and most extensive evils of human history. When men finally realize what they are about, Paul at least wants to be on the side of all human life, even in its least form.

It seems that much sense of human value and worth can be had from Paul VI's controversial document if we attempt to see it in the larger context of the trends of scientific development, of birth prevention, the meaning of genetic control of man, perversion, and population fear as a means to justify any action against human sexual dignity. Taken out of the narrower basis upon which it is read in many religious and secular circles, it becomes clear that serious life issues are here involved whether we like it or not and that the trend of the document is in conformity both with scientific development and with the dignity of human sexuality which is really what is at stake.

There is a serious danger to sexuality in the modern world, and I suspect that we are failing as a civilization to see its nature and proportions. It would be both sad and supremely ironic were an elderly Pope to be the main defender of sexuality itself. I sometimes think God would like to play such a joke upon our pride and intelligence.

What Paul has insisted upon is surely foolishness to the wise. The lesson of the next fifty years will be to see if the present wisdom of the wise turns to foolishness, for what greater foolishness would there be than to sacrifice sexuality itself in the name of sex? That we are in some danger of doing this is paradoxically one of the great realities of our time. Almost the only one who gives us some caution is the Sixth Paul.

Social Thinker

5

People aspire to free themselves from need and dependence. But this liberation must begin with an interior liberty which they must regain before their material goods and their power. Otherwise — we have seen it happen much too often — even the most revolutionary ideologies will obtain only a change of leaders. Once established in power, the new leaders surround themselves with privilege, limit liberty and permit the establishment of other forms of injustice.

Into the Papacy come the problems and worries of mankind; the absolute state, the wars of our time, the threats to love and the family, poverty and discontent. Paul VI has confronted the men of our time with God and with their own failures, with proposals to improve our care of the destitute and the young, the old and the weak. Yet, the man has a sense of finiteness, of the limits of the possible. He seems to realize that our time is overly ideologized.

As I walked into Saint Peter's on a truly beautiful Sunday morning in the middle of May back in 1971 I saw a strong, handsome black. He stood out even in that huge, incredibly varied crowd because he was wearing tight orange pants, with a very shiny orange leather jacket to match, a purple turtle neck sweater, and jack boots. His companion was a white girl with long jet-black hair. She was quite beautiful, dressed in an ankle-length, pure-white gown, almost like a wedding dress, which indeed it may have been.

The lights of the great basilica were being turned on. Next to me, near the front, just below the cameras of the TV and newsmen, was a young woman with a copy of *Europe on Five Dollars a Day* tucked under her arm. Her red-bearded husband was trying to take a photo of the strikingly craggy face of an old worker across the way. His camera was a Yashica.

Behind me, some French women were jabbering about whether the Mass would be in Italian. It would be. A group of wildly dressed, unshaved young Italian boys were loudly consulting one another on how to photograph the brilliantly lighted altar with the wonderful Bernini baldacchino. Their camera was a Kodak. Somehow, I thought, Saint Peter's is always much larger than Saint Peter's!

Paul VI came down the main aisle that morning just after ten, perhaps a bit behind schedule. Everyone applauded warmly. He responded with his usual shy, yet appreciative smile. He was walking —which meant that practically no one not actually on the central barricades could clearly see him. The much criticized *sedia gestatoria*, which he did use on the way out, really is a useful thing after all, I realized, especially if you happen to belong to that 99% of the human race *under* six foot four inches tall!

The Mass was beautiful and simple. In his brief homily, the Pope said it was a commemorative ceremony to recall the Eightieth Anniversary of the publication of Leo XIII's famous social encyclical *Rerum Novarum* (15 May 1891). For the occasion, Paul had just issued his second major social document, to be known, as is the custom, from its first two Latin words, *Octogesima Adveniens*.

This new exposition is not technically an "encyclical" (that is, circular) letter addressed to all members of the episcopacy, or of the Church, or of mankind, but rather an "Apostolic Letter" directed to a single individual in his public capacity, in this case to the Chairman of the Pontifical Commission on Justice and Peace, the Canadian Cardinal Maurice Roy.

Papal Social Tradition

A long and significant series of documents have been issued by the six Popes since Leo XIII on social, political, and economic matters. While noting that there are also numerous and important letters, speeches, and encyclicals of various sorts not here included, the major corpus of modern papal social thought would include:

Leo XIII	1881	*Diuturnum* (On Civil Government)
	1885	*Immortale Dei* (The Christian Constitution of States)
	1888	*Libertas Humana* (On Human Liberty)
	1890	*Sapientiae Christianae* (The Chief Duties of Christians as Citizens)
	1891	*Rerum Novarum* (The Condition of the Working Classes)
Benedict XV	1914-20	Various Peace Initiatives during World War I
Pius XI	1931	*Quadragesimo Anno* (Reconstructing the Social Order);
	1931-37	Letters to Italy, 1931, (*Non Abbiamo Bisogno*),
	1933	to Spain, (*Dilectissima Nobis*),

	1937	to Germany, (*Mit Brennender Sorge*),
	1937	to Russia, (*Divini Redemptoris*),
	1937	to Mexico, (*Nos Es Muy Conocida*), all on the totalitarian governments.
Pius XII	1939-58	*Summi Pontificatus,* 1939, (On the Unity of Human Society) Regular Christmas, Easter, and occasional addresses on Democracy, War, Peace, Technology, Property, Coexistence.
John XXIII	1961	*Mater et Magistra* (Christianity and Social Progress)
	1963	*Pacem in Terris* (Peace on Earth, Modern State)
Vatican II	1965	*Gaudium et Spes* (The Church in the Modern World)
	1965	*Libertas Religiosa,* (Religious Liberty)
Paul VI	1967	*Populorum Progressio* (On the Development of Peoples)
	1971	*Octogesimo Adveniens*

The general topics treated in these letters cover the major public issues of modern times—war, peace, labor unions, just wages, family, nationalism, nationalization, totalitarianism, property, depression, technology, economic development, religious liberty, civic order, world and religious organization, religious values.

Yet, while these documents are almost always issued in response to some current political, economic, or international crisis, they profess to be and are basically *religious* documents. They point out that political and economic problems have inevitably spiritual dimensions. They recognize that man and his explanation involve more than his politics and his economics.

In this sense, the most fascinating and consistent elements in these documents are precisely their endeavors to be more than secular analyses such

as might be found in a collection of the official statements of the Chairman of the Soviet Communist Party or in a collection of the State of the Union Addresses of the American Presidents since 1890.

The memory of the Holy See—as Lord Macaulay already pointed out in the last century—is, in fact, very long, much longer than any other political or social body in the modern world. Likewise, its scope is much broader than any single nation or continent. Whether there be a special value to historical vision, universality, or spirituality is not always easy to judge. Yet, there is no doubt that the modern world has failed, when it has failed, largely because it has neglected one or the other of these aspects of the life of man.

Christian Pragmatism

The second social document of Paul VI has been called "Christian Pragmatism." And this is a good description of it. We are in a period in which most ancient and current intellectual schemes for world betterment and human meaning have been found seriously wanting in productively human results. Indeed, most of the loudest criticism of *Octogesima Adveniens* comes from those sources that can somehow still convince themselves that they are able to grasp the whole mystery of man and the cosmos in their own small, usually rather dirty hands.

For the all-embracing schemes and philosophies —from classic liberalism, to socialism, to communism, to totalitarianism, to existentialism, to recent mystic revolutionism—papal reaction has always shown a healthy skepticism. Yet, this skepticism about ideology has constantly been counterbalanced by a great faith in man, in a belief that he is always much greater than his self-contained systems.

Christianity does not conceive itself as a utopia nor as an ideology, with the result that it can bear a healthy, even maddening patience towards those ever-recurring political and philosophical positions which claim to be able to explain and cure all of mankind's ills.

Utopia and ideology can sometimes have, as the Letter notes, a certain critical function with regard to freeing ourselves from the ills of a given present. But we are already at a late date in history. Far too many utopias and ideologies have become actualized only, in their concrete performance, to restrict and disappoint man in some new and usually frightening way. Our age is, in many ways, tired to death of ideologies. In a real sense, Paul's *Octogesima Adveniens* is a remarkable witness to this mood.

The reflection of Paul VI in his second social document repeats the long tradition of opposition to socialism, liberalism, and communism as intellectual theories, a criticism begun even with Pius IX and then with *Rerum Novarum,* to be repeated and expanded in later encyclicals.

Many see this repetition as mere intransigence or superfluity. Yet, the abstract theories of socialism or liberalism or communism hang about even though they are clearly not the answers to life's mysteries or problems or politics. To expect a Pope or anyone else to proclaim that they are, is merely naive. The experience of the past eighty years, it strikes me, has, if anything, shown the Popes more right than wrong in their analyses of what would happen if such systems should gain control.

Furthermore, it is perhaps worth noting that the masses of people are usually considerably behind the philosophic moods of a given period. I.M. Bochenski has remarked:

> Two great laws appear to condition the opinion of the masses in regard to philosophy. On the one hand, the acceptance of the public is always extremely slow. Thus a philosophy that has flourished fifty or a hundred years ago has the greatest chance of becoming popular independently of the esteem it may have among philosophers themselves. On the other hand, the public can resist much less than the philosophers the double attraction which belongs to the simplicity of a system and the way it is presented.[1]

In a sense, the full force of these approximately one-hundred year old systems is just reaching the masses, especially those newer peoples who have not seen in context the vast philosophical background out of which they arose. And the papacy in the religious sense is necessarily much concerned with the needs of the vast majority of peoples as they actually are being affected by various governments and movements. Socialism is à la mode in the Third World and most South American revolutionaries define European and American business as Nineteenth Century liberalism. This alone is enough to explain why the classic modern movements and ideologies again appear in the present document of Paul VI.

Octogesima Adveniens, too, is at pains to distinguish the various types of marxism — 1) an active practice of class struggle, 2) a collective exercise of political and economic power under the direction of one party which controls all aspects of life, 3) a socialist, materialist ideology which denies any transcendence, and 4) a presumed form of rigorous scientific-critical method to rationalize history and apply the theory to world transformation.

There is little doubt, however, that today the intellectual foundations of marxism and socialism have about run their course so that their theoreticians are in a state of almost intellectual stagnation, while the practitioners respond more and more with something like the Brezhnev Doctrine—that is, with force pure and simple.

And it is more and more thinkers like Solzhenitsyn from within this system that testify most graphically to this ideology's bankruptcy. Zbiegenew Brzezinski has thus written:

> Until a few years ago, the Soviet Union represented for many radicals an appealing and innovative social experiment. This is hardly the case today. Though revolutionary radicalism is gaining strength in Latin America and South Asia, modern radicals, by frantically searching for relevant utopia's in Cuba, China, or even Algeria, bear silent testimony to the proposition that communism in power has become an essentially conservative force, reflecting the concerns and the concepts of an earlier age.[2]

The theoretical analysis of a movement must be kept in tune with both the intellectual viability of the theory and its actual political power. The two may not at all be the same.

Judgment by Practice

Paul VI's *Octogesima Adveniens* should be read in the context of a weariness with ideologies, and with the difference between what they claim and what they do. Paul continues to analyze and to condemn communism and socialism as theories of man. Yet, at the same time, the papacy continues to keep contact with various marxist regimes in the sphere of diplomacy.

Major communist leaders like Marshal Tito visit the Vatican. There is a concordat with Poland and Bulgaria. The increasing Communist Party power in Italy itself has given rise to new relationships and problems. The authoritative Italian journal *La Stampa,* watching these moves, was worried that the game of the Italian Communist Party has been precisely to produce in Italy a type of Church-State arrangement modeled on that of Eastern Europe, so that Italy could one day pass into the Eastern orbit with hardly a notice.

> Preserving in Italy the concordat, namely a certain type of preferential relationship between church and state, our communists—who see in the distance much better than their adversaries—project an even greater similarity between our state and those of Eastern Europe, especially Poland, which laboriously tries to elaborate new concordat formulae to overcome the many obstacles and arrive at a possible co-existence—we should say armistice—between church and state.[3]

The papacy as a religious organization is more than willing—some would say, too willing—to achieve some kind of practical accommodation with communist states so that a minimum of religious life might exist.

Is this merely opportunism and cynicism? John

XXIII, as we have seen, said in *Pacem in Terris* that there was a difference between ideology and social movements in history based upon ideology. Abstract ideas as such do not change. Social movements of men may. And like men, they may change for better or for worse. Which way they are actually going demands empirical evidence—pragmatism, if you will—not abstract speculation.

But this also calls for the courage to call spades spades, to judge objectively both improvements and deformations according to some criterion of the true needs of man. In the post-war years, but more especially recently under the impact of the Russian and Eastern European dissidents, all governments, not just the Holy See, have come to see the greater necessity of frankness in recognizing what ideologies *do* do, not just what they *hold*.

Paul VI has repeated the practical attitude of John XXIII. He has been very down-to-earth with regard to existing historical ideologies, even the worst. This seems opportunist and maddening to doctrinaire purists of the right or left. But in terms of the way the Church conceives herself and man, it makes good sense.

In a very real way, the French Revolution and Napoleon still govern modern times; and of all institutions, the Church is the least likely to have forgotten the lessons of that era. For the French Revolution was an absolute theology of government, rooted in the correction of real abuses and laced by more than its fair share of fanatics, which had to be ultimately replaced, even eradicated, by a shrewd, pragmatic dictator, who had some broad sense of the needs of the people and the nature of the times.

That the contemporary world is still full of such forms of governmental histories, goes without saying. After the overthrow of the Duvalier regime in Haiti, *The Economist* noted that any realistic analysis of the world finds many more depressing regimes than we are likely to admit:

> The real explanation of the unpleasantness of the Duvalier regime is to be found in the nature of power and in the way power was organized in Port-au-Prince; and this is why Haiti is not the special case that many people find it conveninent to believe it is. There are plenty of other small, backward, tucked-away countries where the conditions of life are not all that different from those of Haiti; they include quite a few of the countries of Africa and Asia, and the odds are that some of them are in the process of producing their own local Duvaliers. There are also some countries which have relatively advanced economies and relatively well educated populations, but which have deliberately created a single center of power as a matter of political principle. It is these one-party states, and particularly those where the single party has taken the economy as well as politics under its control, which have the most reason to be looking uneasily at Haiti and the marxist states—the differences in literacy levels, and income per head, and the rest of it—are much less important than the similarity between them when it comes to the structures of power.[4]

The subsequent arrival of Idi Amin in power and the discovery of Gulag would tend to confirm this. As Daniel Moynihan pointed out, in a most unpopular statement, objectively speaking there are only a couple of dozen real democracies in the world today.[5] *Octogesima Adveniens* shares much of this realism:

> Today, men aspire to free themselves from need and dependence. But this liberation must begin with an interior liberty which men must regain before their material goods

and their power. They will never succeed without a love that transcends man and consequently without an effective openness to service. Otherwise, we have seen it happen much too often, even the most revolutionary ideologies will obtain only a change of leaders. Once established in their turn in power, the new leaders surround themselves with privilege, limit liberty, and permit the establishment of other forms of injustice.[6]

It is this concrete attitude, able to see clearly what does happen with even the most exalted theories that can keep public life open and human.

The Church does not see itself as a political institution, nor a state, nor a government. To make such a claim for itself would be heresy even in Christian terms. The Church feels that its religious message and life need to be and have a right to be present in any form of political society, no matter how perfect or no matter how corrupt. This is why Paul is willing to be pragmatic even in the face of the greatest political totalitarianisms. Consequently, religion must be perceptive of the actual ways the events of an era are in fact going.

If our generation insists upon embracing some kind of absolute ideology, as well it might in spite of it all, the Church as an organization must consider how it can, in some perhaps desperate way, live in such a world. There is a kind of grim realism in religion that requires its presence at man's most tragic moments. Not without reason is the last man at the guillotine the chaplain.

One of the constant social messages religion must bear to mankind in whatever his historical condition is that this world is not enough for man and that it is indeed passing away. As men, we never much like to hear this reminder, which is probably why it is necessary from time to time. Paul VI, in any case, has seen that his main religious function is to keep this truth present.

The New and the Old

If we are to note anything new in *Octogesima Adveniens* it is, in a sense, the consistency with which this anti-ideological pragmatism comes through. *Rerum Novarum,* for example, laid great stress on the rights of labor to organize and seek a just wage. *Octogesima Adveniens,* on the other hand, sees modern labor unions not so much in terms of their ideal rights, but in terms of their actual effects on the common good which is larger than the interests of the unions themselves.

There seems to be a disappointed worry that contemporary unions have too often been willing to sacrifice the public interest to their own organizational self-interest. The problem of urbanism is seen to be the primary modern context in which social life is lived. There is a kind of resigned admission that agriculture must become a modern industry if mankind is to be properly cared for. Ecology is mentioned but, as is typical of non-American writing, it is seen as subordinate to the primacy of man and his needs in the world. There is perhaps too little appreciation of many of the non-Christian ideas behind much of the ecological movement.

Echoing many contemporary slogans, moreover, there is an exalted notion of participation and equality in this Letter. They are seen as the contemporary expressions of human dignity and liberty. A wide sharing of responsibility is seen as the primary counterbalance of too much power. *Octogesima Adveniens,* however, brings up again a theme begun by Pius XII about the fundamental problems connected with modern scientific thought and technology, a theme that has subsequently gained much attention. John XXIII and Vatican II had taken an attitude of basic benevolence towards science so that they left aside, for the most part, any thoroughgoing criticism of them.

While he does not reverse this approach, Paul VI is more in tune with the anti-scientific and anti-technological criticisms of recent years. Man has become the object of his own sciences. The sciences certainly have their own legitimate spheres of competency. But man is himself not merely a scientific object, and the total sum of science and technology does not add up to all that man is.

Arthur Koestler's recent notion of "dynamic wholes" seems to be a sign of a similar consciousness of the need to look at science and man in a more complete fashion.[7] For Paul VI, man is not and cannot be a pure object of scientific analysis or manipulation. But this position can only be maintained, the Holy Father argued, if man is more than the object of his own studies.

There is a certain type of wild optimism and liberalism in this kind of religious thought typical of the Pope which defies science and technology in the name of mankind in the very act of insisting on their essential contribution to human welfare. In this sense, the papal anti-scientific and anti-technological criticism is again pragmatic in its analysis of what in fact science and technology can and are doing. Thus, the paradoxical event comes about that it is more and more religion that finds itself the main defender of science's legitimacy and need in a world more and more doubting both science and technology.

The Anglican theologian Eric Mascall has, with his usual perception, noted the subtle temptation to which official religion is often exposed in recent years, namely the easy identification of religion with pure social action in the world. This is, in a way, the neglect of an old truth of religion, of Christianity, and it is a most severe problem for Catholics especially because of the vehemence and urgency with which developmental problems—of which Paul wrote in *Populorum Progressio*—are being brought up everywhere.

Paul VI rightly observed that one of the basic functions of religion is to be open to and conscious of the needs of the poor in any age and place. This is a theme he had often repeated in his pontificate. It is also clearly a basic function of religion to be where the poor are. Yet, as Mascall suggested:

> As I see it, modern man has been starved by his social and cultural environment of the objects of two of his most fundamental needs, the need of community and the need of transcendence. In the past few centuries the Church tended to satisfy the latter need at the expense of neglecting the former; now the wheel has come full circle. With the recovered consciousness of the essential corporate nature of the liturgy and of the Church as the Body of Christ one must enthusiastically agree, but the question may be asked whether there has not gone together with this a loss of the consciousness in the

> loving will of a transcendent God, in whom alone man can find ultimate satisfaction and who alone is the adequate object of his devotion and wonder. Unless we can recover the sense of transcendence in our worship, our concern with the passing needs of our human contemporaries is doomed to frustration. Neither in the roman nor in the anglican communion is the danger absent of an attitude which is so involved with human welfare that the basic justification for this involvement falls out of view.[8]

In other words, there is a real danger today that the cries of revolution, development, and ecology will conquer the religious mind to such an extent that its central function of witnessing to something beyond man will be obscured.

Not without reason, Eric Mascall has feared that already within the secular world itself the cry and need for mysticism has begun to be heard. Indeed, it is manifest on every side. If religion should in its turn be identifying itself with social action and revolution alone, it would be tragic. It would leave the rising mystical fervor among us without theological depth. And this has always been a most dangerous thing for society.

Bochenski's thesis about social philosophies is of some moment here, for the classical ideologies are about one hundred years old and their intellectual life is quickly dying. Thus, if there is any basic weakness in *Octogesima Adveniens,* I suspect, it lies here, with the generally imperfect notions Third World and European theorists have of the newer mystical and anti-scientific movements now arising.

In a sense, the most necessary parts—even politically—of this second social letter of Paul VI are the spiritual and religious ones. Indeed, as we shall see in the next chapter, undoubtedly the most important thing about Paul VI is precisely his own concept of the faith, his own spiritual outlook and vision. For what we need to know most about is not a Pope's view of the world, but his view of God.

Figure of Faith

6

The idea of a God Who needs no one, Who has created us freely out of love and Who searches for mankind in an active manner, lies behind Paul's notion of prayer and the Christian religion. Prayer is a searching for God but, as we have learned as far back at least as St. Augustine, it is not a one-sided affair.

Any Pope must be a public figure, a well-known person of the times in which he lives. Normally, the Holy Father will be the most widely recognized religious leader in the world. He will be expected to be a man knowledgeable in God's ways, but he will also be expected to know a good deal about the condition of the world.

Many of the reasons why a Pope will be known to the world, of course, will arise from issues and problems that are especially popular, tragic, or controversial. What he does on Christmas or Easter usually will receive widespread coverage. What the Holy Father thinks or says about politics, economics, war, or sex will be, for better or worse, issues that will define much of his popular image.

This is not bad, certainly. Paul VI, moreover, has insisted upon taking a stand in public when he thought it advisable or necessary. He has not waited for the world to come to him either, though that is, in a sense, the way he normally communicates. His pontificate has seen him travel widely within Italy, in Europe, Latin America, the United States, Africa, Australia, and Asia. Paul VI has been no "prisoner of the Vatican."

Furthermore, he has been a remarkably productive Pope—as much as Leo XIII, Pius XI, or Pius XII, the latter of whom may still hold the record for papal productivity. Are there, then, I often wonder, any characteristics or stresses that would serve to differentiate Paul's own particular approach to the faith as it is to be lived and seen by men in our time? He has, in fact, displayed a deep and intelligent spirituality which deserves more than passing attention. He has also manifested a persistence in keeping before Christians and the world just what it is the faith fundamentally consists in.

He has sometimes been criticized for not being strict enough with those theologians and clerics who would downplay or interpret away basic elements of faith and doctrine. I suspect he has simply taken seriously the notion that a Pope should reprimand mostly as a father and teacher, a method that may often leave the problem itself unresolved. In any case, in his addresses, letters, and encyclicals, he has made a remarkable case for the validity of the Christian faith and practice in its fundamental historical outlines, a case that bristles with uncommonly accurate knowledge about what the current and classical objections to the Christian religion are.

View of Papacy

The very first thing to be noted about Paul VI —and this is a direct challenge that he makes in and by his person—is that he firmly believes himself to be the Pope of Rome and the Successor to Peter. He believes that his main task is to make sure that the essential core of the faith is clearly understood in his time and passed on intact to the next generation. Paul knows that he is merely a human being, fallible and finite in so far as he is Giovanni Montini. He makes no pretense to be worthy of the office, and there is little doubt that this sentiment is genuine. But neither does he think that particularly matters. His remarks at his Coronation Homily must be taken at face value:

> First, then, in spite of our misgivings, we venerate the hidden ways of God who has willed to commit to our feeble strength a burden so immense, so priceless as his Catholic Church.... To us, God has entrusted this Church; to keep it holy, to make it prosper. But that is not all. He demands of us, as he has always demanded of all his Vicars, that we give our every thought and care, and if need be life itself, to the extending more widely among men the Church's divine, inexhaustible resources of spiritual power....
>
> Heavy indeed is the burden that is laid upon our shoulders—a burden that will overwhelm us but for our reassuring conviction of God's power. For his greatest works, he often chooses instruments that by any human reckoning are wholly worthless.[1]

These are rather disconcerting words since it is not often we are confronted with the real thoughts of the human person who does bear the Keys of Peter.

Nine years after his Coronation, Paul recalled to a General Audience some further personal reflections on his papacy. He realized that the primacy might be an obstacle to some, that the task of being a shepherd with both love and authority must be a difficult one. But his reminiscence on his becoming Pope are worth much reflection since Paul is most conscious that it is the hand of the Lord that really rules.

> Let us tell you, very simply, about an impression of ours connected with that day (his election to the papacy), and still present in our mind. We seemed to feel overwhelmed by the playing out, whether mechanical or mysterious, of an event above and beyond our will. We had never in the slightest way desired—far less promoted—our election.... On the contrary, the previous service we had carried out humbly and for long years under Pope Pius XI ... and then under ... Pope Pius XII, had made us only too well acquainted with the enormous mass of duties, difficulties, and needs which St. Peter's keys bring with them, and too aware of the preparation necessary for this formidable office, not to recognize our lack of the charisms required for such a burdensome ministry.
>
> In this regard, we find the following among some of our personal notes: "Perhaps the Lord has called me to his service not because of any aptitude of mine, not to govern and save the Church from her present difficulties, but to suffer something for the Church, and to make it clear that he, and no one else, guides and saves her." We confide this sentiment to you not to make a public and therefore vain act of humility, but in order that you also may enjoy the tranquility which we experience in thinking that it is not our weak and inexperienced hand at the helm of Peter's boat, but the invisible, yet strong and loving, hand of the Lord Jesus.[2]

And the following year, to the College of Cardinals, he said of his ten years as Pope: "We have sought only the glory of his name, only the expansion of his kingdom, the progress of his Church, the transmission of his word, the proclamation of his truth and his peace."3 Now if Paul VI were a Julius II or an Alexander VI, we might be more inclined to pass all this off as mere rhetoric. But I suspect he is quite sincere in these personal remarks about his own mission and what the Church conceives it to be.

Undoubtedly in these years of doubt and theological controversy about the office of the papacy itself, it may come as a shock, indeed a healthy shock, to realize that Paul VI believes himself to be what the Roman Church dogmatically holds him to be. In the case of his office, Paul has consistently showed himself genuinely aware of what he is as Pope, as Bishop of Rome. He has not apologized, somehow, that the papacy is a necessary office in the Church, of divine origin. He is considerate of ecumenical problems which his office might cause, but he is quite concerned about Catholic critics who do not always support him.

In 1968, he remarked to the College of Cardinals:

> Certainly we cannot remain silent about the sorrow it causes us to see our intentions and even our words misunderstood or distorted at times; nor about the fear that a certain number of sons—fortunately few, but still too many as far as we are concerned—and through their efforts, others who are less firmly grounded and more vulnerable, will depart from the right path....4

And of his office itself, he explained at the Angelus in 1973:

> Peter was placed at the head of this plan, which is called the Church, or the means of salvation.... Today, many people tend to say: Christ, yes, we accept him; but the Church, no. Others say, Yes, there is need for a Church, but not that of Peter. With what historical, evangelical or charismatic authority can they assert this? How can they remain

> with Christ and in Christ while prescinding from the bond of unity with him and among ourselves, which was established by him?
>
> As far as we are concerned, let us seek humbly, faithfully united to Peter, and we will be united to the Church, with Christ, with the divine life that comes from him alone.[5]

Paul VI sees his office as an active, positive position. But also, it is one that must explain and exercise itself for the good and authenticity of the Church.

Perhaps the most difficult and delicate letter he has written in defence of the Church from criticism within itself was to the Dutch Bishops in 1969, regarding certain ideas about Catholic doctrine which he felt needed to be corrected there. Paul first listed the objections he found in Holland. He then suggested his willingness to do what is helpful to them, but he reminded the Bishops that the principle of solution was to be found in the historic content of faith which is his and theirs to uphold and hand on.

> Permit us, in our turn, to offer some remarks ... for your pastoral attention.
>
> 1) In the matter of ministerial office: a) the description of the purpose and tasks of the Church is presented as if her mission were merely terrestrial; b) the priestly ministry is looked upon as an office conferred by the Christian community; c) a proposal is made—and sometimes in a very persistent fashion—that the priesthood be disassociated from celibacy; d) criticism is directed against the position that only men can become priests; e) whenever mention is made of the Pope, it is always to minimize his office and the powers conferred upon him by Christ himself.[6]

Paul in such a delicate context wonders what he may do, but concludes with the central principle that governs all his approach to Christianity:

> It seems to us that in the face of these currents ... while keeping in mind the fundamental distinction between the deposit of faith and the way in which it is expressed, your attention should be directed most of all to the implications of your basic office as teachers of Christian doctrine, which means your duty to transmit in all its integrity the content of revelation, of which the Church is the depository.[7]

All of these actions and reflections of Paul on his office serve to emphasize the first thing that must be realized about him—that he believes what his office says it is and that the central deposit of faith will be guarded and passed on, for this is what men need and desire above all else. This is what is unique about the faith and justifies its existence. This fidelity too marks the spirituality of Paul VI.[8]

Paul on What Christians Believe

We have seen previously that the Pope has taken considerable pains to associate himself with the problems of mankind of our era, especially those concerning the poor and weak and innocent. Both on humanist and Christian grounds, he has held consistently that technical, economic, political, and social issues are not within the direct competence of the faith. However, many of the disorders and evils arising in these areas were precisely ones rooted in moral or religious values.

He accepted without hesitation the thomistic notion that the natural order was itself good and with its own autonomy, though that order was derived from God as creator. Paul wrote to Professor Etienne Gilson, the great scholar of Christian medieval thought:

> You have demonstrated the originality of Thomism by showing how the Angelic Doctor profited by the light of Christian revelation (especially the doctrine of creation and what you yourself have called "the metaphysics of Exodus") to reach the original and really revolutionary idea of the "act of being" (*ipsum esse*). By that very fact his philosophy stood on an entirely different plane than that of Aristotle. You have thus unsealed once more a fountain of wisdom from which our technological society can derive great profit, for it is a society fascinated by "having" but often blind to the meaning of *being* and to its metaphysical roots....
>
> ... (Another) important idea that is especially dear to us ... is the idea that faith does not enchain or extinguish human thought and culture but is a light and a stimulus for these.[9]

He has also consistently believed that charity, justice and mercy were the virtues that ought to govern men's relations. And he has held that Christians, like all men, would be especially judged by what they have done for the poor and the least of their brethren. The Christian religion is also directed to men in this world in their work, art, pleasures, culture, and accomplishments.

This being said, lest there be any doubt about Paul's concern in this area, it must be recognized that Christianity is a religion with a view of a divine plan for men and that the primary purpose of this plan is not terrestrial. The philosophical primacy of *being* over *having* and the religious primacy of *God* over *creation* serve to ground the Christian in a reality already there, already perfect, in God.

Both the best and the worst public social orders still leave untouched in themselves what religion is essentially about. And it is this religious truth above all that Paul VI has insisted on preserving and presenting to men. He believes, to be sure, that much of the disorder in the socio-economic world does have religious roots. But he does not believe that the first purpose or justification for religion, least of all Christianity, is to improve the world. To take this position is already to rule religion out of the discussion. This insistence of the Pope is often a difficult doctrine for the modern mind to accept. But the Christian view of man is only justified if it can speak to men in *other* than terms of worldly accomplishment.

Throughout his pontificate, Paul VI has made sure each year that the principal part of his teachings, talks, and instructions be concerned with what is unique dogmatically and devotionally about Christianity so that men learn to know and pray and practice this "good news" in their lives.

The liturgical year, of course, fosters the occasions to speak of the Nativity, the Resurrection, Pentecost, the Virgin, the Saints. Paul VI has spoken long and often on faith, joy, penance, prayer, vocations, priesthood, religious life, obedience, sin, mysticism, hope, mercy, justice, and love. The significance of these papal efforts, their spiritual significance, can easily escape us if we see in the Pope only a political figure, only someone trying to find a place and a position in the affairs of this era.

He is concerned, vitally concerned about the temporal problems of men. No one who reads his *Populorum Progressio,* his *Octogesima Adveniens,* or his innumerable addresses on public issues can doubt either his concern or his comprehension of these areas. Yet, when all is said and done, he remains what he says he is: the Pope, the Pastor who must care for the spirit of his flock, teach, urge, inform, remind. He is a religious figure who believes that God has revealed himself in his triune life to the world. In a sense nothing else really matters.

Undoubtedly, he has tried to make it clear that man's relation with God is the essential thing about man. And this relationship takes precedence of and endures within any political, economic, historical, or social condition of the men who have existed and do exist on this planet. In 1968, at the closing of the Year of Faith, Paul wrote a remarkable *Profession of Faith* that deserves much more attention than it has received. In a way, it would be difficult to find a better statement of what religion is about.

> We confess that the Kingdom of God begun here below in the Church of Christ is not of this world, whose form is passing, and that its proper growth cannot be confounded with the progress of civilization, of science or of human technology; but that it consists in ever more profound knowledge of the unfathomable riches of Christ, an ever stronger hope in eternal blessings, an ever more ardent response to the love of God, and an ever more generous bestowal of grace and holiness among men.[10]

In understanding both Paul and the faith he represents, it is important, to begin here, since the most important heresy in modern times is precisely the elevation of worldly prosperity and order to the highest mission of men, or put another way, the identification of Christian eschatological dogmas with political ideologies. Paul VI has consistently refused to do this and in so doing has guaranteed the true nature of Christianity, whatever be the form of earthly regime.

God

Throughout his years in the Vatican, Paul has paid a good deal of attention to God. He has endeavored to talk about God, about the reasons for believing in Him, the objections against believing, together with the difference God's reality, and belief in it, makes in our lives. Back in 1970, while he was at Castel Gandolfo for the Summer, Paul gave a series of six lucid "chats," to the General Audiences each week that are quite important in understanding the Holy Father's spiritual outlook. He began his first address this way:

> Let us talk about God for a while. Or rather, let us talk about ourselves confronting the great question of God. We ask you to perform this act which is fundamental for our thought, and consequently for our moral life, for the lives we lead. It is a permanent question, existing at all times and applying to all people, but today it is more urgent. Let everyone ask himself: What do I think of God.[11]

What is remarkable about this address, indeed the whole series—"Can We Know God?", "Why Worry About God?", "Is God Out of Date?", "Other Values in God's Place?", "How Can We Seek God?", and "Can We Find God?"—is the Holy Father's comprehension of the complexity of the question and his willingness to talk about God to the ordinary kind of persons who might come to an audience. For Paul, God is not just for the intellectuals or religious—even though he is for them too. There is a kind of abiding personalism in the Pope which confronts men with God even though no one else is doing so. This he sees as his main task.

In a subsequent Letter Paul addressed to the

Vatican Secretariat for Non-Believers, he explained why a theoretical humanism, which would exclude God, is not enough.

> ... We believers have no doubt about this conviction: a humanism that is closed upon itself and that excludes God will sooner or later prove to be inhuman. Why? Because God remains the origin and end of the supreme values without which man cannot live; because the realities of sin and death, and the questions they pose for the individual and history, receive no definition or complete solution apart from faith.[12]

The Pope reaffirms again and again the central Christian belief in the existence of God, His absoluteness and completeness, His being before all reality was. But it is important to understand what this means. God is not a process coming to be, but He already is, independent of ourselves and our history and our universe. This is, in fact, the crucial truth about God that relativizes all else and defines the meaning of personal human life.

"And more than that, just listen: Suppose that God Himself should be in search of us? Isn't this the mysterious and sovereign plan of the history of our salvation?"[13] For Paul VI this active search of God is not a supposition; it is in fact what goes on, what gives human life, which he has been at such pains to defend, its ultimate meaning and value.

When he speaks of God and about His existence, knowability, and nature, he does not intend to limit Himself to our rational knowledge. Paul refuses to believe that reason is so weak that it cannot know God in a beginning way. On the other hand, the important thing about this God is what

He has revealed about Himself and the relation of man and earth to Him.

The two essential doctrines of Christianity about God are that He is Trinity and that the Second Person, the Son, became man in time. On 8 March 1972, the Congregation for the Doctrine of the Faith published a Document reaffirming the meaning and centrality of these truths about God. It did so because some were teaching, evidently, views contrary to what the Church has held.

Regarding the Incarnation, some appeared to doubt that "the Son subsists from all eternity in the mystery of the Godhead, distinct from the Father and Holy Spirit." Others, further, "abandon the notion of the one person of Jesus Christ begotten in His divinity of the Father before all ages, and born of the Virgin Mary in time." And, finally, there is the position that the humanity of Christ was not assumed into the Second Person, but "existed rather of itself as a person, and therefore that the mystery of Jesus consists only in the fact that God in revealing Himself, was present in the highest degree in the human person of Jesus."[14]

The Trinity, the doctrine of the internal life of God is held to be revealed in Scripture and to be basic to Christian belief. Many apparently doubted the eternity of the Trinity and wondered if the Holy Spirit were a distinct person. Paul VI made some interesting remarks about this Document at the Angelus on 12 March 1972. He noted something that others, such as Chesterton, have noted: that the denial of the most basic elements of the faith, especially those dealing with God, has far reaching effects on man in the world.

> During the past week, amid the hubbub of exciting but not always edifying events on the world scene, the Church raised its voice to defend two fundamental truths of our faith: the unity and trinity of God and the divinity of Jesus Christ....
>
> Owing to a mentality which has spread even among us believers, who are today less sensitive to doctrinal questions, not much attention may be paid to this important act of the ecclesiastical magisterium which reaffirms the brightest and most august truth of Christian revelation. But the faithful ... should have a vivid spiritual realization of the great importance of this frank safeguarding of the supreme mysteries of our creed....
>
> Accustomed as we are to assessing everything in terms of subjective utility, it is possible that some may wonder whether such dogmas are useful for the solution of the many pressing problems besetting our immediate concrete experience. We would answer, first of all, that religious truths are in themselves supreme and inestimable values, worthy of our homage and attention. Secondly, looking at things correctly, it is precisely from adherence to religious truths, now safeguarded for our Catholic conscience, that we can draw applicable, operable principles for the theological, ecumenical, ecclesial, spiritual, and even social and practical problems which burden our minds, shaken by so many interior and exterior difficulties. It is precisely from firm and fervent faith in this God—one in being, triune in Persons, through whom we have been baptized and joined in Christ, God and man —that we can draw light and love for a truly human solution to life in all its aspects.[15]

Paul VI has been quietly persistent in keeping the Trinity and the Incarnation at the focus of our religious life. It is this God in His revealed inner life that justifies all else about Christianity.

Redemption

If the Pope has centered his spiritual thought on God, consequently, he has seen human life as a personal relation to this God through the revelation he has given men of Himself. This means that the primary drama of human life has to do with our personal response to this revealed God. This justifies and grounds the place the Church has ever given to personal prayer, to the contemplative life, to silence. In a sense, this is the first need of the world, that the dignity of the person through the Incarnation can pierce directly to God, the very beginning and end of all else.

In 1970, Paul made Catherine of Siena and Teresa of Avila Doctors of the Church. Both of these women were very active in their time, each dealt with political issues of great importance. But it was their prayer and mystical contact with God, its possibility and reality that served to define their real Christian importance.[16] Whenever Paul VI speaks of prayer, it is with the sense that it reaches an active God, concerned in the now of the person in his time.

But there is a plan of our salvation. Because of the freedom of men in their self-definition of their destiny, this plan includes the Cross, sin, suffering. Paul VI has ever and calmly reminded us of the relation of the Incarnation to these facts of our being, which he feels we all can recognize if we will.

There is a good deal of talk, with which the Pope is familiar, about "the new man" that is supposedly necessary or actually coming to be.

Such a phrase as "the new man," of course, has scriptural overtones. The specifically Christian approach to this problem can best, perhaps, be seen in two wise passages of Paul concerning the religious understanding of man's situation and what it is that ultimately satisfies him—that is, life with God and this alone. In 1968, Paul told a General Audience:

> The Christian ideal begins with the known premise of the dignity of man and his perfectibility, but is based at the same time on a twofold negative observation. The one derives from man's inheritance of original sin, which has weakened his very nature, giving rise to a lack of balance, to deficiencies, and to weakness of faculties. The other denies the ability of human power alone to reach true perfection which is necessary to man's salvation, namely the sharing in the life of God through grace.[17]

There are two things to emphasize here—the reaffirmation of the importance of original sin and the recognition that our ultimate destiny is first a gift of God quite beyond our power of self-attainment.

The importance of original and actual sin in Christianity is well known. Because of them, Christianity consistently rejects plans and programs that would seek to save men—that is, promise them some kind of perfect happiness—by their own means. Moreover, beyond that, Christianity holds, in the second passage, that the end to which man in fact is destined is personal in his autonomy but with God in his Trinity along with those who share the life of God. To the 84th German Katholikentag in 1975, Paul wrote:

> To wish to limit the responsibility of Christianity to the service of men and the world merely to the economic, social

and cultural spheres would mean betrayal not only of the Church's real mission, but also of man himself. Man's complete human development requires necessarily the religious dimension. The real evil that enslaves and threatens man is not this or that unjust social system, this or that social need, but sin, man's alienation from his creator. Even if men were to succeed in creating an earthly paradise, eliminating all enslavement and all poverty, he would still need God's saving message above all, and the Church would have to proclaim to him God's salvation in Christ.

Therefore, in the Christian social service of man and society, it is essential to preserve and emphasize the fundamental feature of the Church's task, which is to be the way, means, and instrument for humanity's supernatural liberation and redemption. More than exterior relationships and structures, it is above all men themselves that must be changed through proclamation of the liberating word of Jesus Christ's good news and through the sacramental rebirth to the new nature created after the likeness of God.[18]

This teaching function of Paul to keep in focus what the Christian religion is fundamentally about has not been an easy one precisely because the alternative to Christianity is a worldly social order that can profess to offer itself as self-sufficient.

The denial of this justifies both the need for Christian evangelization and for the religious reality God is in the world. The Pope reiterated this in his Address on "Evangelization and Human Progress," the theme of the 1974 Synod.

It will be necessary to define more accurately the relationship between evangelization properly so called and the whole effort to world development, for which the Church's help is rightly expected even though it is not its specific task. We are aware of the objective difficulties encountered in this regard by the Church's sons and daughters who are dedicated to apostolic work. Very often today they are urged to forget the necessary priority of the salvation message and to restrict their own efforts to mere philanthropic, sociological or political activity, and the scope of the Church to a man-centered, temporal message.

> Hence the need to restate clearly the specifically religious aim of evangelization. It would lose all its significance if it were to diverge from the religious fullness that sustains it: the Kingdom of God before anything else—the Kingdom of God in its fully theological meaning, which frees man from sin, and proposes the love of God as the greatest commandment and eternal life as the ultimate destiny.[19]

The thought of Paul VI on Christianity is firmly based upon this religious aspect of the redemption which is the thing men, of whatever society, are most in need of knowing.

Faith

The challenge that Christianity gives to men is not merely that they are rational beings whose powers of knowledge are valid, but that the complete knowledge of what they are presupposes a non-contradictory faith. "Let us remember, dear children," Paul told a General Audience,

> "that during our earthly life it is not given to us to 'see' divine reality, but to 'know' it; and even this knowledge derives not from natural and ordinary knowledge, but from faith.... The mystery of salvation is communicated to us in two ways: the objective way of the word of God—which subjectively, means faith—and the way of sacramental action. To these ways we may add a third, the Church...."[20]

He further told the Episcopal Conference of Africa, "The faith must always be the principle guiding your action and the supreme motive for the Church's activity in society. For, in point of fact, the specific nature of the Church's salvific mission is irreducible to something purely and simply of the temporal order."[21]

Faith is what grounds the Christian in that kind of salvation that was given to him, one that involves the Cross and suffering, one that does not falsely promise their elimination but their sanctification. The Christian does not believe that men will not eventually be happy if they choose in faith, but it does patiently insist that this world is largely a vale of tears and that to promise or preach otherwise would only be to delude.

> For the person who believes in Christ, the troubles and sorrows of this present life are signs of grace, not misfortunes.... We know, in fact, that in virtue of the redemption all the defects inherent in human nature, or deriving from the wounds of sin and left in us for the time being as a reason for asceticism and conformity to Christ crucified, will be removed on the day when God "shall wipe away every tear from their eyes, and there shall be no more death or mourning...."[22]

The Cross and the Resurrection are seen to be intimate elements of the faith for Paul. Both are very real, both directly pertain to the person of Jesus and through Him to us in our own personal lives. Both sorrow and joy are Christian but this results from the faith in the kind of salvation we have been given and from this alone. And out of this comes the only real hope that counts, the hope that deals with our own personal destiny. This is why resurrection remains the test of the Christian faith.[23]

Prayer

Paul VI views God as a personal, triune reality who has created men in this world to share His inner life. What happens in the world, what men do with it and to each other in their freedom is important, but the world and the human city is not and cannot be man's highest destiny. The real drama is the redemption and the vital activity of the transcendent, triune God. The priorities are to be, "Seek ye first the Kingdom of God and then all these things will be added unto you."

The Pope sees that prayer, the personal relation and contact of men directly with God, is the most important thing they can do. Furthermore, prayer is not a one-sided thing. Indeed, grace and redemption mean that God first seeks men in the intimacy of their own personhood. It is interesting in this context to point out that Alexander Solzhenitsyn, in his absolute demand that men never cooperate with evil, insists that only God will sustain them when all else is taken away. In a way, he has forced the modern mind again to confront, in a way not unlike Paul, the priority of the transcendent God over all earthly systems.

In an Address to Italian College Students at Castel Gandolfo, Paul brought up the unaccustomed but theologically most pertinent truth that God takes care of his message, as it were, he is not merely a passive creator.

> We are confident too that the same God who is forgotten, insulted and denied by so many, and whom others would like to regard as dead and buried, is defending himself and our salvation. Infinitely good as he is, he has a counter-

> balance ... to apply to minds that have gone blind.... He is present: He sustains our fallen condition.... God knows how to draw good out of evil.... What is the Gospel, what is the coming of the word of God in our flesh, if not the search by God for mankind?[24]

This idea of the God who needs no one—and therefore who has created us freely out of love, not necessity—searching for mankind in an active manner lies behind Paul's notion of prayer and the Christian religion. Prayer is a searching for God, but, as we have learned as far back at least as Augustine, it is not a one-sided affair. God also searches, because we are in fact free.

The importance of this notion to Christianity can be seen by Paul VI's constant discussion of prayer for the mystics, saints, religious, and ordinary Christians. He is especially convinced that the contemplative life of the Church retain its witness to the sufficiency of God alone. In writing to the Bishop of Lisieux of Thérèse, Paul insisted:

> In our age, intimacy with God remains a primary but difficult objective. The finger of suspicion has been pointed at God. Any attempt to seek him for his own sake has been qualified as an alienation. A largely secularized world tends to cut off human existence and human activity from their divine source and goal.[25]

What Paul regards as his own duty in this matter, his bearing witness to the Christian tradition, is to maintain that we ought to seek God for His own sake, that we are not cut off from the divine Being and action searching precisely for us.

There is, in fact, a widespread phenomenon in the world today of a renewed interest in and recognition of the need for prayer. This prayer, however sincere, has often taken the most bizzare and unexpected forms. In his Apostolic Exhortation on Religious Life, Paul noted the place of prayer:

> Many people, including many of the young, have lost sight of the meaning of their lives and are anxiously searching for the contemplative dimension of their being. They do not realize that Christ, through his Church, can respond to their expectations. Facts of this kind should cause you to reflect seriously on what men have the right to expect of you.... Be aware then of prayer's importance in your lives and learn to devote yourselves to it generously. Faithfulness to daily prayer always remains a basic necessity for each one of you.[26]

Behind this notion of prayer lies the Christian doctrine of the human person, the notion that each one in his very uniqueness is being sought by God, that each one is free to respond to God or reject

Christ

"Who Is Christ?" In a remarkable series of General Audiences—five in 1971 and two in 1974— together with innumerable other Christmas and Easter addresses, the Pope has familiarly and clearly explained who the Church believes Jesus is.[28] He has a lucid and kindly way of presenting Jesus to his listeners. He never lets them forget, indeed he reminds them that they know that Jesus is the Christ, the Second Person of the Eternal Godhead, who became man.

In the Christmas Address of 1973, "The Feast of Christian Humanism," Paul reviewed the hopes

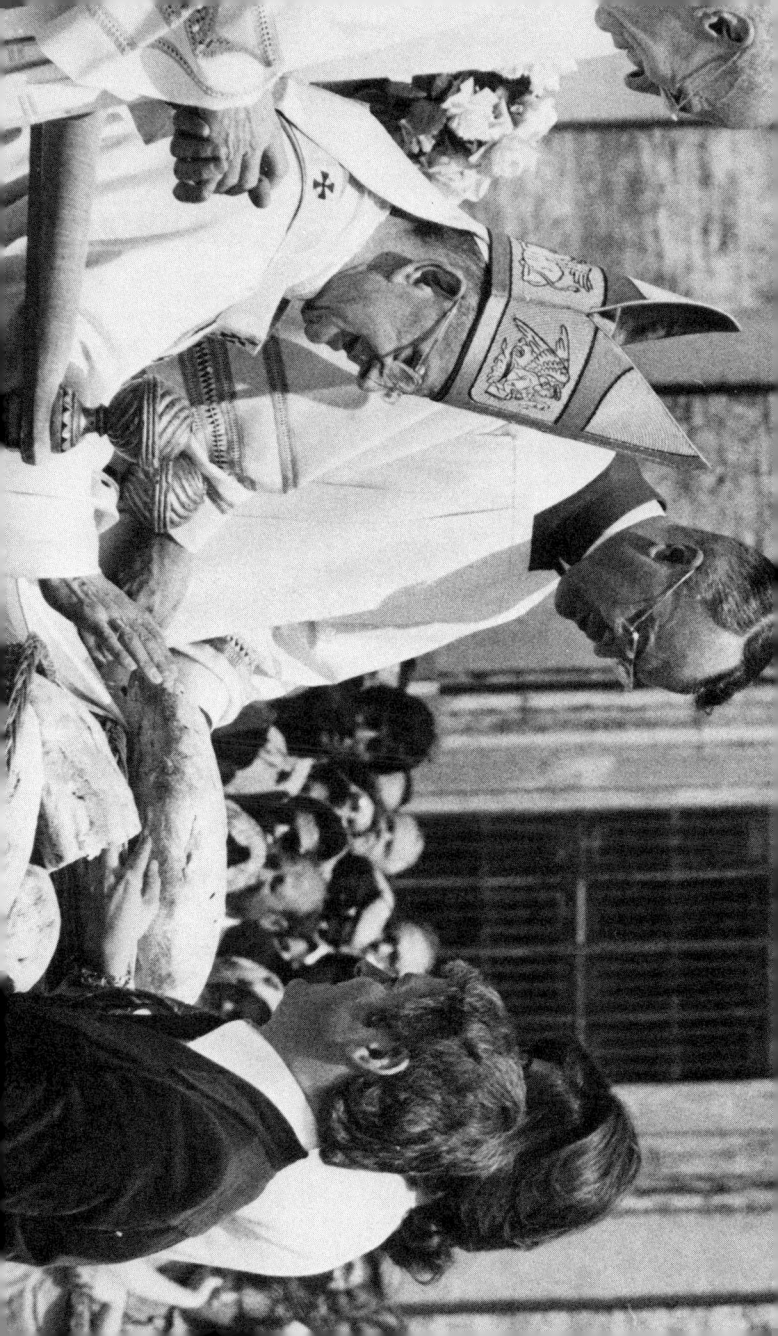

and claims of modern humanism to explain all by virtue of man's own capacities. Many see the human side of Christ alone in this context. Indeed, anthropology often substitutes for theology. There is a persistent belief or search in the modern world that would seek to discover the perfect man in the perfect society. This desire is something that religion recognizes. Yet, the Christian response to this is also a humanism. "It is the message of Christmas, a message that from a son of the human race salvation comes to mankind. The insistent question arises: Is man saved by man?"[29]

In response to this, Paul recounted the core of modern humanist efforts to explain man without recourse to God. Christian humanism, on the other hand, has its roots in man's higher origin, in his dominion on the earth, his fall, his freedom.

> This is man. Woe to the person who interferes with him, for man is born sacred for life, from his mother's womb. He is born ever endowed with the precious but divine prerogative of freedom. This freedom can be trained, but it is inviolable. Man is born as a person sufficient in himself, yet needing social companionship; he is born a thinking, willing being, destined for good but capable of error and sin. He is born for truth and love....
>
> As he exists, man is not perfect. He is a being essentially in need of restoration, rehabilitation, fullness, perfection, and happiness. His is a life which does not suffice to itself; he needs a complement of life, an infinite complement. Exalt man, and you will make more obvious his deficiency, his incompleteness, his inner need to be saved. We say it directly and in a word: Man needs a Savior.
>
> Yes, man needs a Savior—a man who will be one with men, but will at the same time be God, so that he may lead man to the level of the divine.[30]

This is a perceptive reflection on the Christian

notion of humanism and the place Christ occupies within it. Christian humanism professes to be and is a humanism that accounts for man's dignity, his evil, his goodness, his hopes, his sufferings, and his call to more than himself.

Who is this Jesus? All of Paul's reflections on Jesus are conscious of Scripture and the Church tradition as well as an awareness of modern scholarship, its strengths and objections. His pastoral reflections are often very spiritual, very much to the point. Modern Christians are often caught between what popular and academic reflections claim about Jesus and the Jesus the Church teaches. Paul is very much interested in this scholarship, even insists upon it, but he is not blind to the fact that some of the interpretations of Jesus are of dubious orthodox origin.

> Here let us close and fearlessly face the storm of Christologies unleashed against our Catholic faith—those of the last century especially, and of today.... Let us admire the extremely erudite effort of modern learning to investigate Christ and his person, his history, and the evidence about him, and let us learn to study more ourselves. But we should be watchful, even distrustful, as we see school succeed school; as we observe that the enormous erudition of so many teachers is usually permeated with some hypothesis, prejudice, or questionable philosophy which, when joined with the wealth of knowledge which they have accumulated, often leads to shipwreck in invincible doubt or radical and irrational denial.[31]

In this context, he has tried to pursue in many straightforward ways the Christ that has been handed on to the Church and Him alone.

> Christ, then, is to be met by each person. Let us think carefully about this meeting with Christ, and in particular

> what it involves for us. Let us consider it in the context of the great religious plan offered to world history. Without leaving heaven, and forsaking the attributes of his eternal divinity, the God of mystery enters the changing scene of time. He who is infinite takes on the limits of *kenosis,* that is to say, he empties himself. He is ineffable, yet he clothes himself in our visible flesh.[32]

This Jesus, God and man, is the personal link to God we all have. The result of His presence is the drama, the choice which defines ultimately the meaning and destiny of each person.

> If, upon reflection, we also discover that this plan concerns us personally, that it is wholly centered on each of us, it becomes our personal drama. It endows us inwardly with an extraordinary wealth of gifts, the gifts of the Holy Spirit; and it offers us a free but formidable choice regarding the kind of life we want to live: are we Christians or not? That is to say, are we Christians or are we, in the last analysis, insignificant beings deprived of eternal hope?[33]

The Pope does not doubt that the life of God in Jesus reaches us personally, nor does he doubt that we as authentic persons have a duty to be open to what we are, a theme he insisted upon in the Council Document on Religious Liberty.

Paul VI's view of Christ is one that is founded on what he was handed by his tradition. The reason for Christ's life as a man is a direct and personal one to each human being. In rejecting a millenarist Christianity, one that would promise a worldly utopia, he realizes that he is defending the personal worth and destiny of each person, no matter in what age or political reign he might find himself in.

> Jesus has been magnificently understood and defined, in contemporary Christological discussion, as "the man for

> others." This is so. And St. Paul—that is, all the theology of the New Testament and of Catholic Tradition—had a deep insight into the secret of Jesus' earthly life, the reason, and the purpose of the Incarnation, and he tells us in what form and to what extent Jesus was for others: "Christ died for our sins according to the Scriptures." (I *Cor.* 15,3)
>
> Jesus came to the world for us and for our salvation. This is what Jesus did: He saved us. He was called just that, Jesus, which means Savior. And he saved us by becoming a victim for our redemption. This is the mystery of abasement of the man Jesus that merges with the mystery of the sublimation of the man Jesus Christ in the Incarnation. It enters into the most important truths of the Christian theological system, that is, into the eternal plan, fully revealed only with Christ, of God's love for us.... For without this mystery, we could know nothing about ourselves. It enters into the sacrificial value of the Lord's Passion, which is universal and replaces the expiation that would otherwise be due from us which would be impossible for us.
>
> Here we have the final and total work of Christ, the Redemption. The Redemption enters into human destinies in such a way as to establish a possible, free and highly auspicious personal relationship of each of us with our Lord Jesus Christ....[34]

The realism of Christianity is absolute in its consistency, in its joining men to the life of God through Jesus Christ in each person's own personal, physical being and life. This is why the resurrection of the body remains at the core of authentic Christian belief.

Joy in the Spirit

The Redemption ends in the revelation of God's love, His inner life which is to be shared.[35] Paul VI, as we have indicated, has never let Christians forget the dark side of their natures and actions.

Evil and repentance and suffering constitute human realities also, and these have a Christian meaning within the faith's overall mystery. The Christian religion ends, however, where it begins in the Trinity, in the final knowledge or Father, Son, and Spirit.

Revelation ends in love and joy. Paul's wonderful Apostolic Exhortation on *Christian Joy* of 9 May 1975 is a refreshing emphasis on the Trinity, its place in our faith, and in the meaning of joy that flows from its reality.

> ... For in his (Jesus') human consciousness he was aware of being the object of the same divine love which is directed to him as God in the bosom of the Father: "... the love you bore me before the world began." (*John,* 17,24)
>
> This love is the mutual love that cannot be communicated because it is identical with the very being of the Son and is the inmost root of the Trinitarian life. For in the Trinity the Father is he who gives himself wholly, uninterruptedly, and with infinite ardor to the Son, while the Son is he who gives himself to the Father in the same way, with an infinite joy and thanksgiving, in the Spirit.
>
> Christ's disciples, and all who believe in him, all called to share his joy.... This joy which springs from abiding with God begins on earth and is proper to the Kingdom of God.... The chief thing the Good News of Jesus Christ promises is joy, but it is a demanding joy.[36]

FOOTNOTES

Introduction

1 George Kelly, "An Uncertain Church: the New Catholic Problem," *The Critic,* Fall, 1976, p. 23.
2 James Hitchcock, "Bigotry in the Press: The Example of *Newsweek*," *The Alternative,* October, 1976.

Chapter I

1 Bruno Bettelheim, "The Uses of Enchantment," *The New Yorker,* 8 December 1975.
2 27 Janvier-2 Fevrier 1969.
3 *Corriere della Sera,* 17 Febbraio 1969.
4 *Herald-Tribune,* Paris, 24 April 1969.
5 27 April 1969.

Chapter II

1 Jean Guitton, *Dialogues avec Paul VI,* Paris, Fayard, 1967.
2 Speech of 14 June 1967. In Paul VI, *Demeurez fermes dans la foi,* Paris, Centurion, 1967, pp. 62-63.

3 *The Pope Speaks* (Hereafter referred to as *TPS*), 14 February 1969, *TPS,* 14-1-1969, p. 50.

4 December 29, 1968, *TPS,* 13-4-1969, p. 324.

5 January 22, 1973, *TPS,* 18-1-1973, p. 72.

6 *Ibid.*

7 *Ibid.*, p. 73.

8 January 13, 1974, *TPS,* 18-4-1974, pp. 357-58. Cf. also speech of 18 April 1970, *TPS,* 15-1-1970, pp. 4-9.

9 Cf. August 10, 1966, *TPS,* 11-3-1966, p. 234.

10 *Ibid.*

11 Cf. the author's "Apocalypse as a Secular Enterprise," *The Scottish Journal of Theology,* V. 29, § 4, pp. 357-73.

12 October 24, 1966, *TPS,* 12-1-1967, pp. 62-63.

13 April 15, 1973, *TPS,* 17-1-1972, p. 5.

14 *Ibid.*, p. 7.

15 April 24, 1968, *TPS,* 13-2-1968, pp. 109, 112.

16 August 6, 1975, *TPS,* 20-3-1975, p. 235.

17 *Ibid.*, pp. 236-37.

18 November 1, 1971, *TPS,* 16-2-1972, p. 346.

19 *Ibid.*, p. 347.

20 November 27, 1972, *TPS,* 17-4-1973, p. 356.

21 May 13, 1972, *TPS,* 12-2-1972, p. 134.

22 Guitton, pp. 159-75.

23 May 17, 1970, *TPS,* 15-2-1970, p. 146.

24 *Ibid.*, p. 147.

25 *Ibid.*, p. 148.

26 December 5, 1974, *TPS,* 19-4-1975, p. 290.

27 *Ibid.*, p. 297.

28 *Ibid.*

29 *Ibid.*, p. 298.

30 *Ibid.*

31 *Ibid.*, pp. 299-300.

32 November 27, 1968, *L'Enseignement de Paul VI,* Paris, SEDIM, 1969, p. 200.

Chapter III

1 Cf. *The Pope Speaks,* 15-2-1970. On 17 May 1970, Pentecost, Paul celebrated his 50th Anniversary of Ordination by himself ordaining some 278 men to the priesthood in St. Peter's. This particular homily is a good example of how Paul

views his own priesthood. One paragraph at least is worth citing: "We feel obliged to thank all, relatives and friends, teachers and fellow workers, those present and those absent, those whom we know and those whom we do not know. We feel moved to summarize our feelings for them in a single autobiographical testimony, which is not original—because every priest can make the same act of witness for himself—but which is true: what a wonderful thing it is to be a priest!" *TPS*, 15-2-1970 p. 142.

2 17 February 1972, *TPS*, 17-1-1972, pp. 55-56.

3 October 13, 1971, *TPS*, 13-3-1971, p. 211.

4 "The mystery of vocations pertains solely to God, and we cannot have any doubt at all that God will provide for the good of His Church, to which He promised His presence and assistance until the end of the world....

The grace of a vocation placed in a soul by God is fundamentally nothing else but a more abundant provision of divine charity, destined for the Church and for building up of God's kingdom on earth. In the times in which we live, it often happens that this grace does not attain its goal. In order that it may do so, favorable conditions must be created —in the minds of the young in a particular way, in the family environment, in the Christian community and in places of training for the priestly and religious life." 12 April 1970, *TPS,* 15-1-1970, p. 11. Cf. also *TPS,* 18-4-1974, p. 343.

5 *TPS,* 16-3-1971, *ibid.,* p. 213.

6 June 30, 1968, *TPS,* 13-3-1968, p. 226.

7 August 24, 1968, *TPS,* 13-3-1968, pp. 243-44.

8 *TPS,* 13-3-1968, p. 226.

9 November 21, 1973, *TPS,* 18-4-1974, p. 343.

10 *TPS,* 17-1-1972, p. 63.

11 February 20, 1971, *TPS,* 16-1-1971, pp. 55-56.

12 August 24, 1968, *TPS,* 13-3-1968, p. 249.

13 February 13, 1972, *TPS,* 17-1-1972, p. 41.

14 *Ibid.,* p. 41.

15 October 6, 1971, *TPS,* 16-3-1971, pp. 216-17.

16 *TPS,* 17-3-1972, p. 202; 18-2-1973, p. 184.

17 June 11, 1973, *TPS,* 18-2-1973, p. 164.

18 *TPS,* 14-1-1969, p. 57.

19 June 30, 1974, *TPS,* 19-2-1974, pp. 163, 165.

20 November 1, 1970, *TPS,* 16-2-1971, p. 122.

21 *TPS,* 17-2-1972, pp. 201-02.

22   *Ibid.*, p. 203.
23   *TPS*, 12-2-1967, p. 115.
24   March 29, 1969, *TPS*, 14-2-1969, p. 129.
25   September 21, 1974, *TPS*, 19-3-1975, p. 207.
26   *TPS*, 11-3-1966, p. 251.
27   *TPS*, 16-2-1971, p. 178.
28   *Ibid.*, pp. 179-80.
29   *TPS*, 12-1-1967, pp. 24-25.
30   *Ibid.*, p. 29.
31   *TPS*, 19-3-1975, p. 235.
32   *Ibid.*, pp. 243-44. cf. also, "Counsels for the Jesuits." 21 April, 1969, *TPS*, 14-2-1969, p. 107-10.
33   December 24, 1969, *TPS*, 14-4-1970, pp. 292-96.
34   April 23, 1972, *TPS*, 17-1-1972, p. 14.

Chapter IV

1   *National Catholic Reporter*, 11 August 1968.
2   The form of *Humanae Vitae* was not stated in itself in the most solemn form open to the Pope.
3   Cf. the author's *Human Dignity and Human Numbers*, Alba House, 1971.
4   Paul VI, *TPS*, 13-3-1968, p. 208.
5   Paul VI, *TPS*, 13-3-1968, p. 207.
6   *Ibid.*, p. 208
7   *Ibid.*, p. 209.
8   Cf. J. Lederberg, "Experimental Genetics and Human Evolution," *The Bulletin of the Atomic Scientists*, October, 1966.

Chapter V

1   *La Philosophie Contemporaine en Europe*, Paris, Payot, 1962, p. 35.
2   "The State of Communism," *Newsweek*, 15 March 1971.
3   "Concordato e Liberta," *La Stampa*, 11 April 1971.
4   "Duvalier Wasn't Unique," *The Economist*, 1 May 1971, p. 18.
5   D. Moynihan, "The Caged Revolution," *Harper's*, January, 1976.

6 Paul VI, *Octogesima Adveniens*, 15 May 1971, *TPS*, 16-2-1971, p. 159. (Variant translation)

7 Cf. G. Steiner, "Life-lines," *The New Yorker*, 6 March 1971.

8 E. Mascall, "The Death of Wonder," *The Way*, January, 1971, pp. 42-43.

Chapter VI

1 30 June 1963, *TPS*, 9-1-1963, p. 5. Cf. also, 23 December 1968, *TPS*, 13-4-1969, p. 308.

2 21 June 1972, *TPS*, 17-2-1972, p. 98.

3 22 June 1973, *TPS*, 18-2-1973, p. 93.

4 23 December 1968, *TPS*, 13-4-1969, p. 308.

5 29 June 1973, *TPS*, 18-2-1973, p. 178.

6 24 December 1969, *TPS*, 14-4-1970, pp. 294-95.

7 *Ibid.*, p. 295.

8 Cf. 11 October 1975, *TPS*, 21-1-1976, pp. 57-59.

9 8 August 1975, *TPS*, 20-3-1975, p. 265.

10 30 June 1968, *TPS*, 13-3-1968, p. 281.

11 22 July 1970, *TPS*, 15-3-1970, p. 223.

12 18 March 1971, *TPS*, 16-1-1971, p. 46.

13 26 August 1970, *TPS*, 15-3-1970, p. 235.

14 8 March 1972, *TPS*, 17-1-1972, p. 65.

15 12 March 1972, *TPS*, 17-1-1972, p. 69.

16 4 October 1970, *TPS*, pp. 196-202; 27 September 1970, pp. 218-222, 15-3-1970.

17 7 August 1968, *TPS*, 13-3-1968, p. 201. Cf. also, 25 March 1970, TPS, 15-1-1970, pp. 22-26; 11 July 1966, TPS, 11-3-1966, pp. 228-35; 30 August 1967, *TPS*, 13-1-1968, pp. 45-46.

18 1 September 1974, *TPS*, 19-3-1975, p. 202.

19 27 September 1974, *TPS*, 19-3-1975, p. 189.

20 14 August 1968, *TPS*, 13-3-1968, p. 205.

21 26 September 1975, *TPS*, 20-3-1975, p. 269.

22 5 October 1975, *TPS*, 20-3-1975, p. 275.

23 22 April 1973, *TPS*, 18-1-1973, pp. 40-41; 4 April 1970, *TPS*, 15-1-1970, pp. 14-17.

24 29 August 1967, *TPS*, 12-4-1967, pp. 350-51.

25 2 January 1972, *TPS*, 17-4-1973, p. 336.

26 29 July 1971, *TPS*, 16-2-1971, p. 124.

THE AUTHOR

Fr. James Schall was born in 1928 and, after graduating from the Knoxville, Iowa, High School in 1945 he did further studies at the University of Santa Clara before entering the Society of Jesus in 1948. He studied Philosophy at Gonzaga University, was Instructor at the University of San Francisco, took his PhD in Political Theory at Georgetown University and was ordained to the Priesthood in 1963. In the following years he completed his studies in America and Europe and in 1965 was appointed Assistant Professor in the Istituto Sociale of the Rome Gregorian University. He regularly teaches in this University but returns each Fall to be Associate Professor, Department of Government in the University of San Francisco.